How Your Body Works!
Anatomy and Physiology

BABY PROFESSOR

EDUCATION KIDS

Have you ever wondered how your body works? This is very interesting. Knowing how our body works helps us understand how to keep healthy.

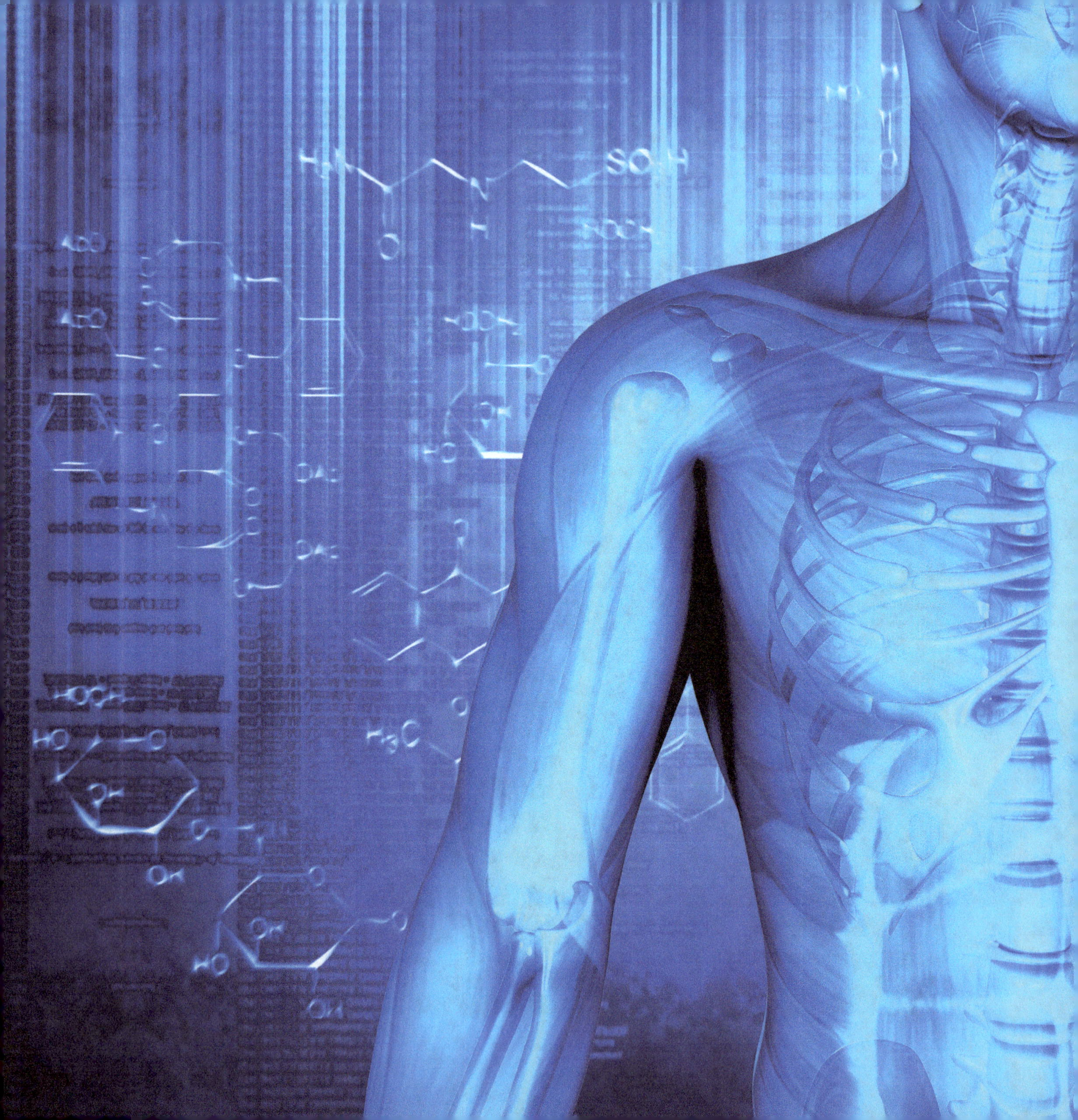

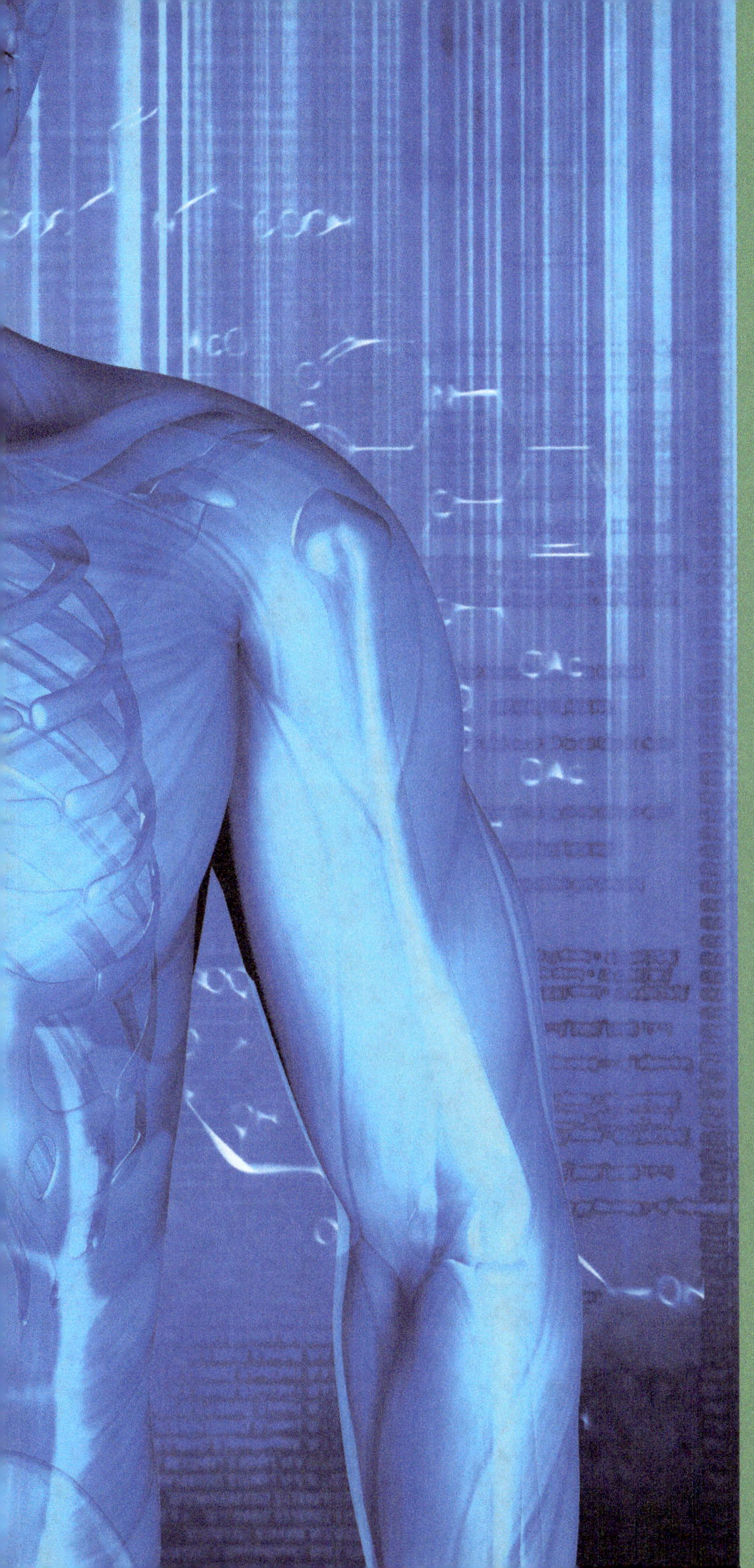

Our body is a brilliant creation. It functions like a high-tech machine which has many important parts.

In this book you
will learn about
different parts
of the body and
their functions.
Let's get into
human anatomy
and physiology!

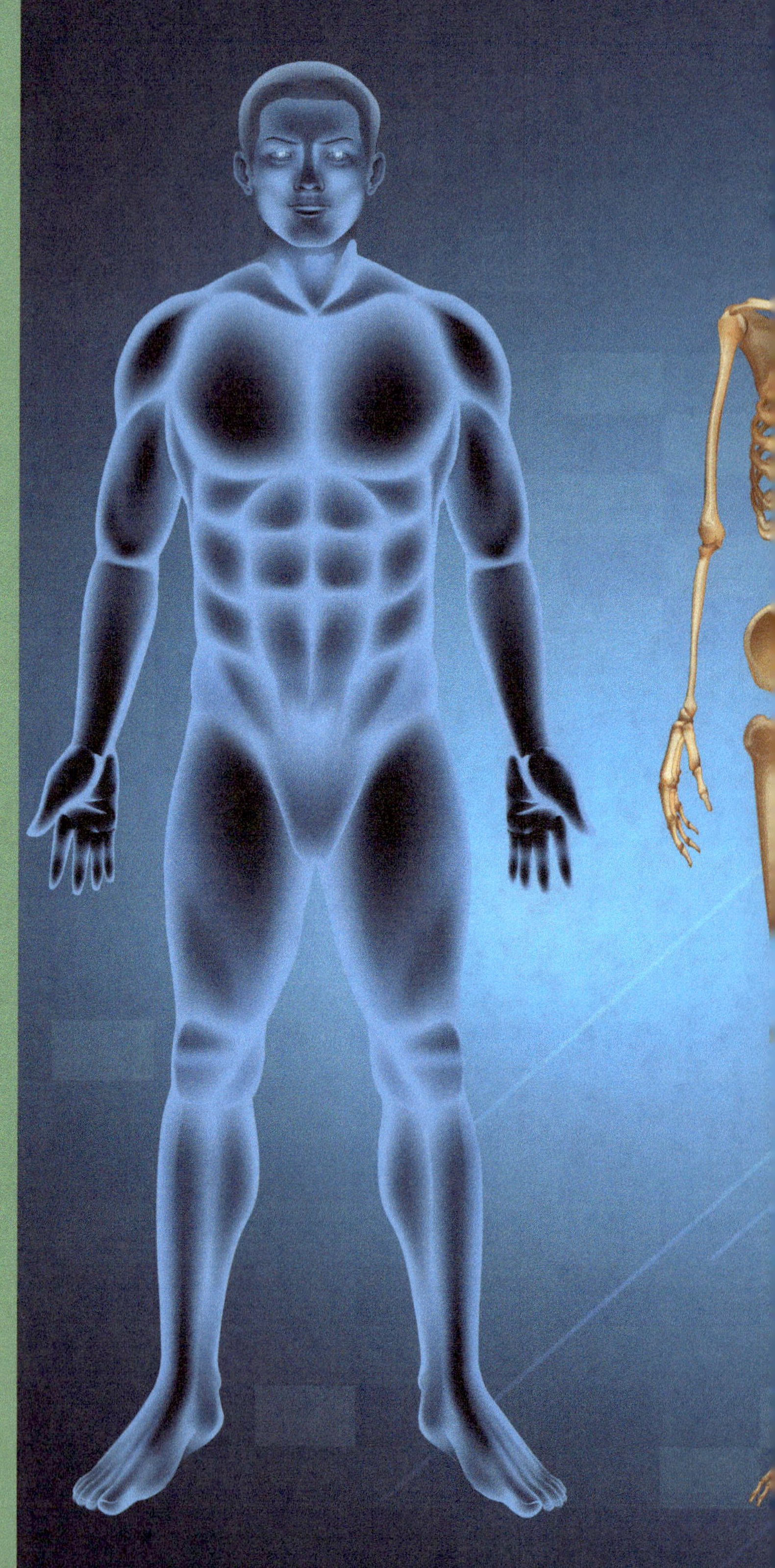

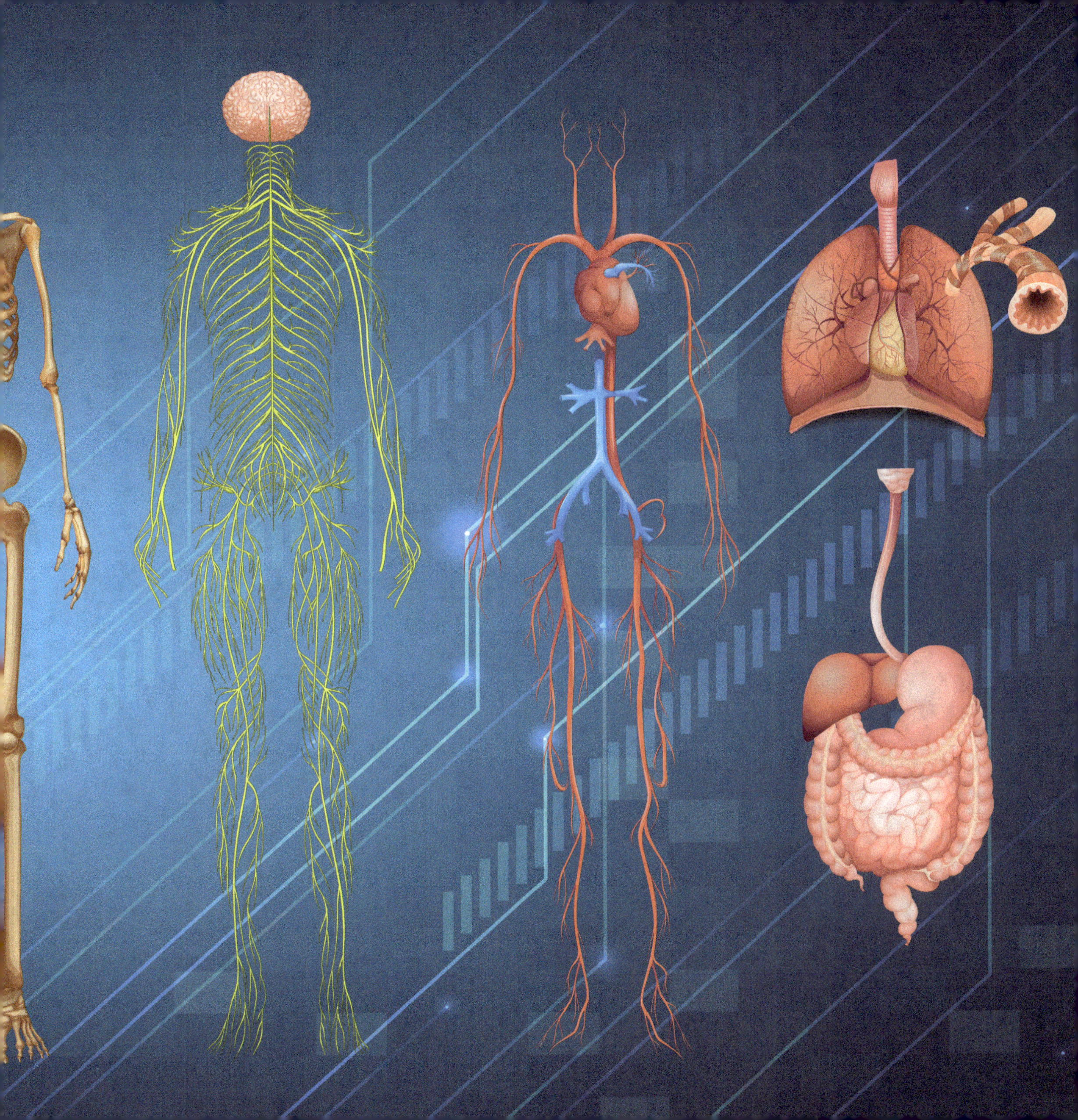

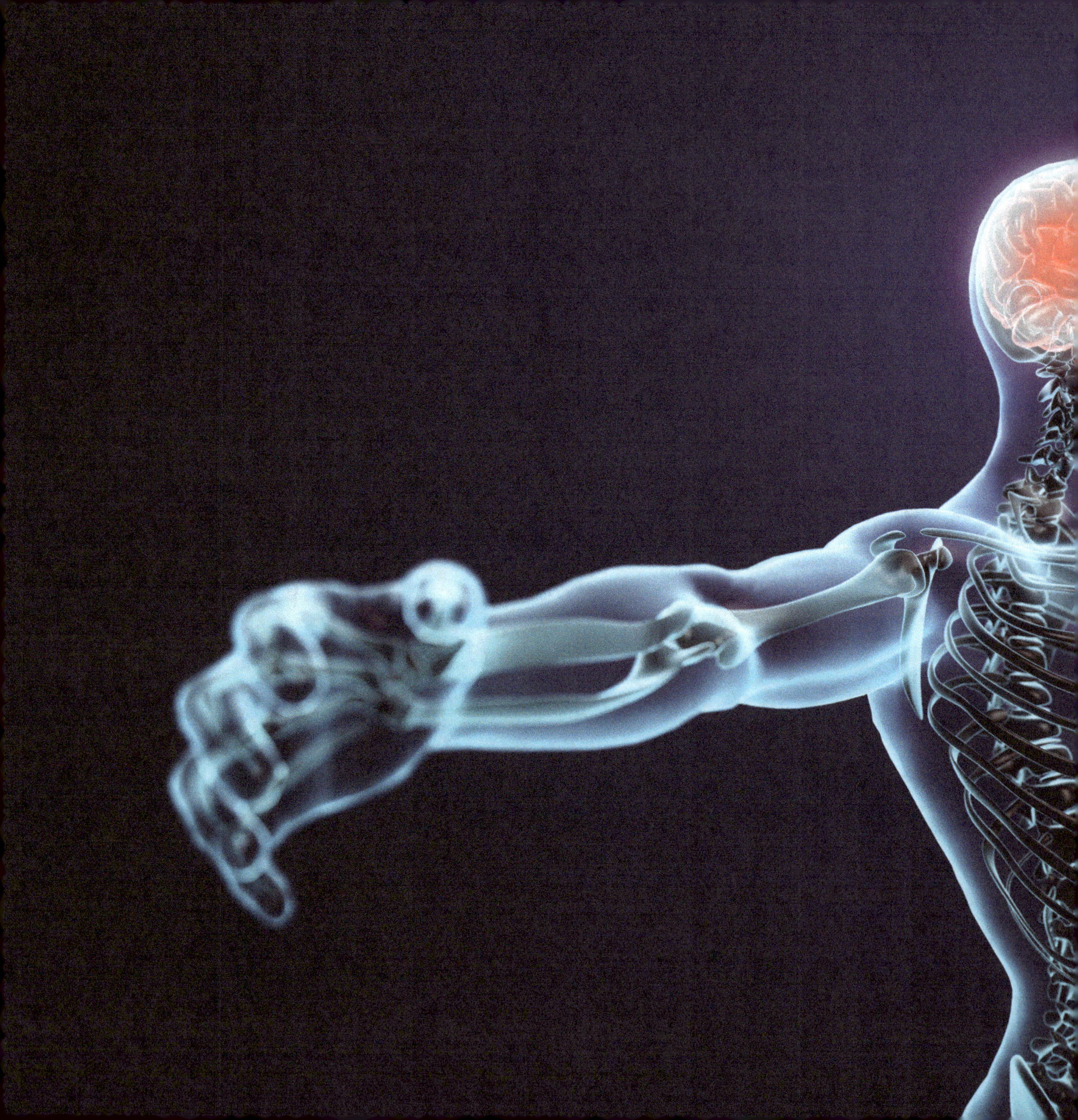

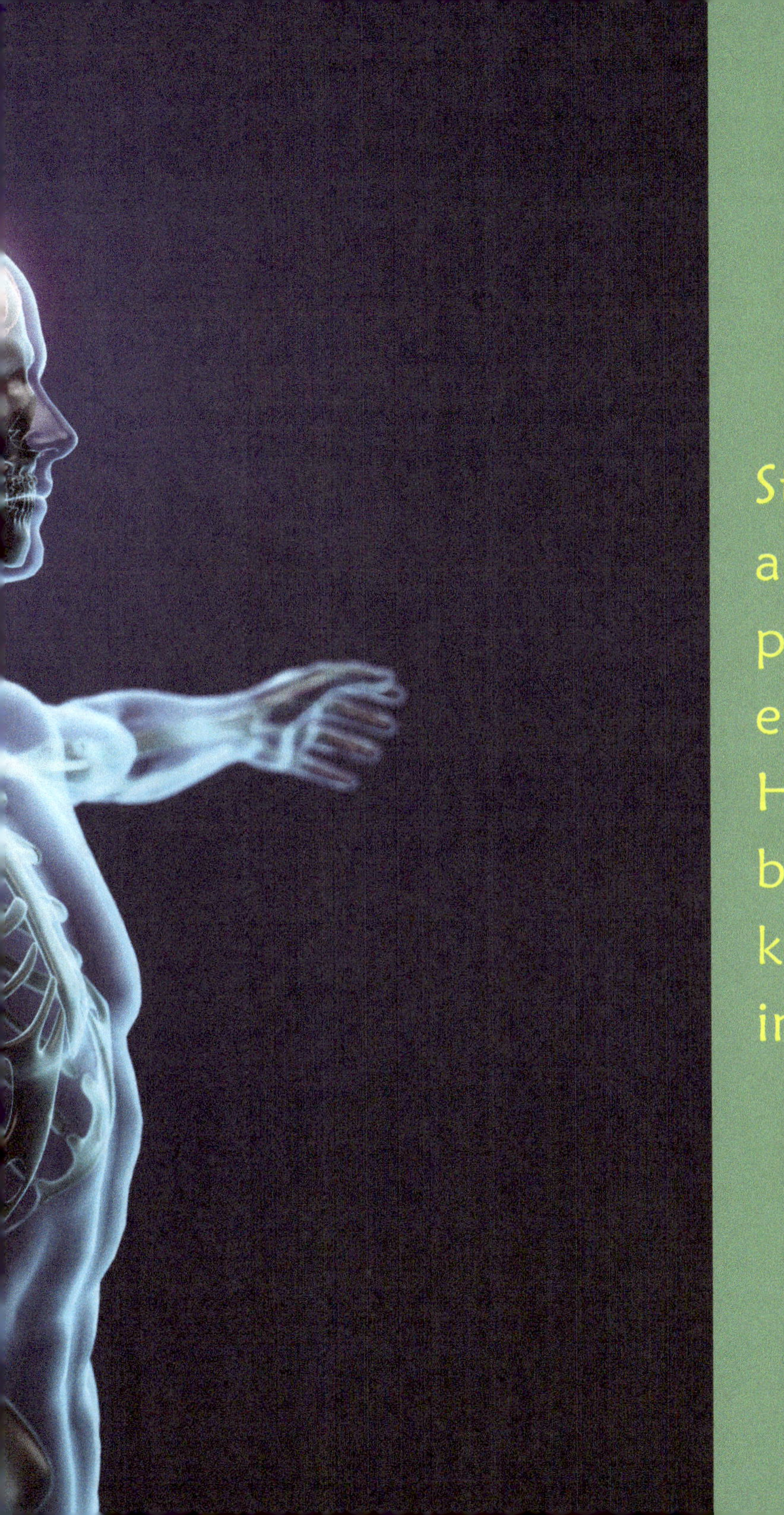

Studying human anatomy and physiology is an exciting journey. How the human body works to keep us alive is indeed fascinating.

By knowing
how our body
parts work, we
can definitely
say that there is
magic within us.

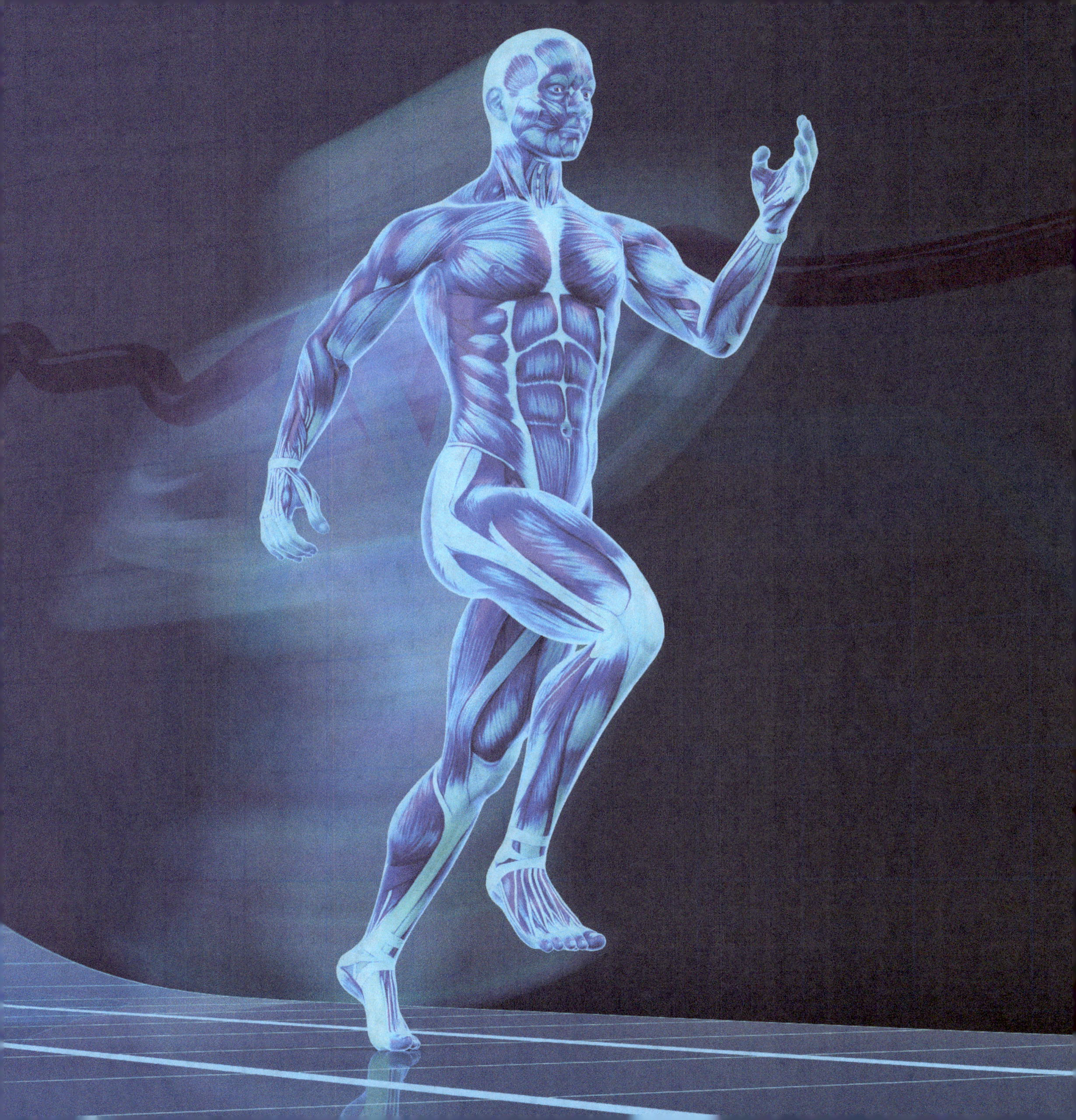

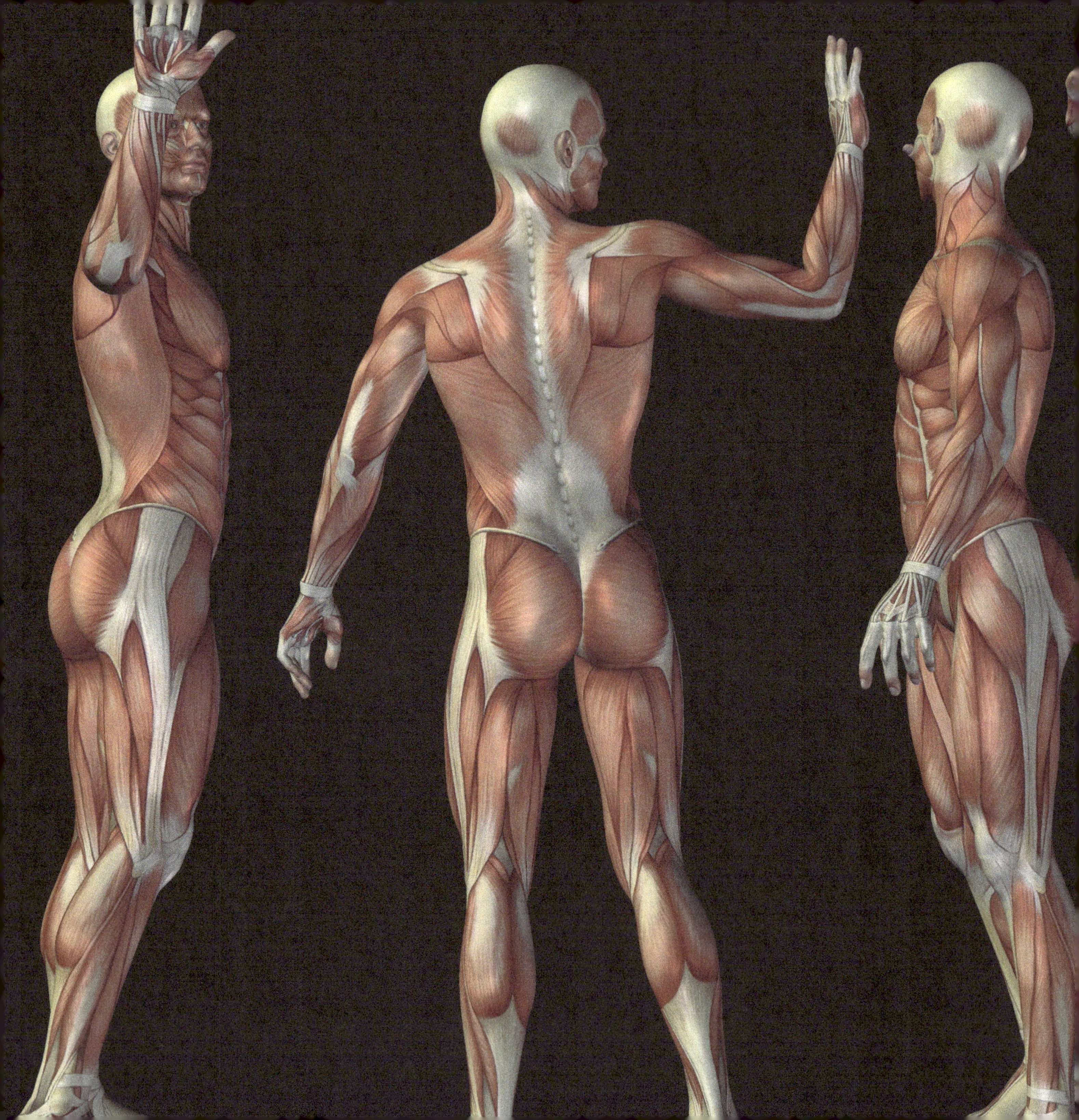

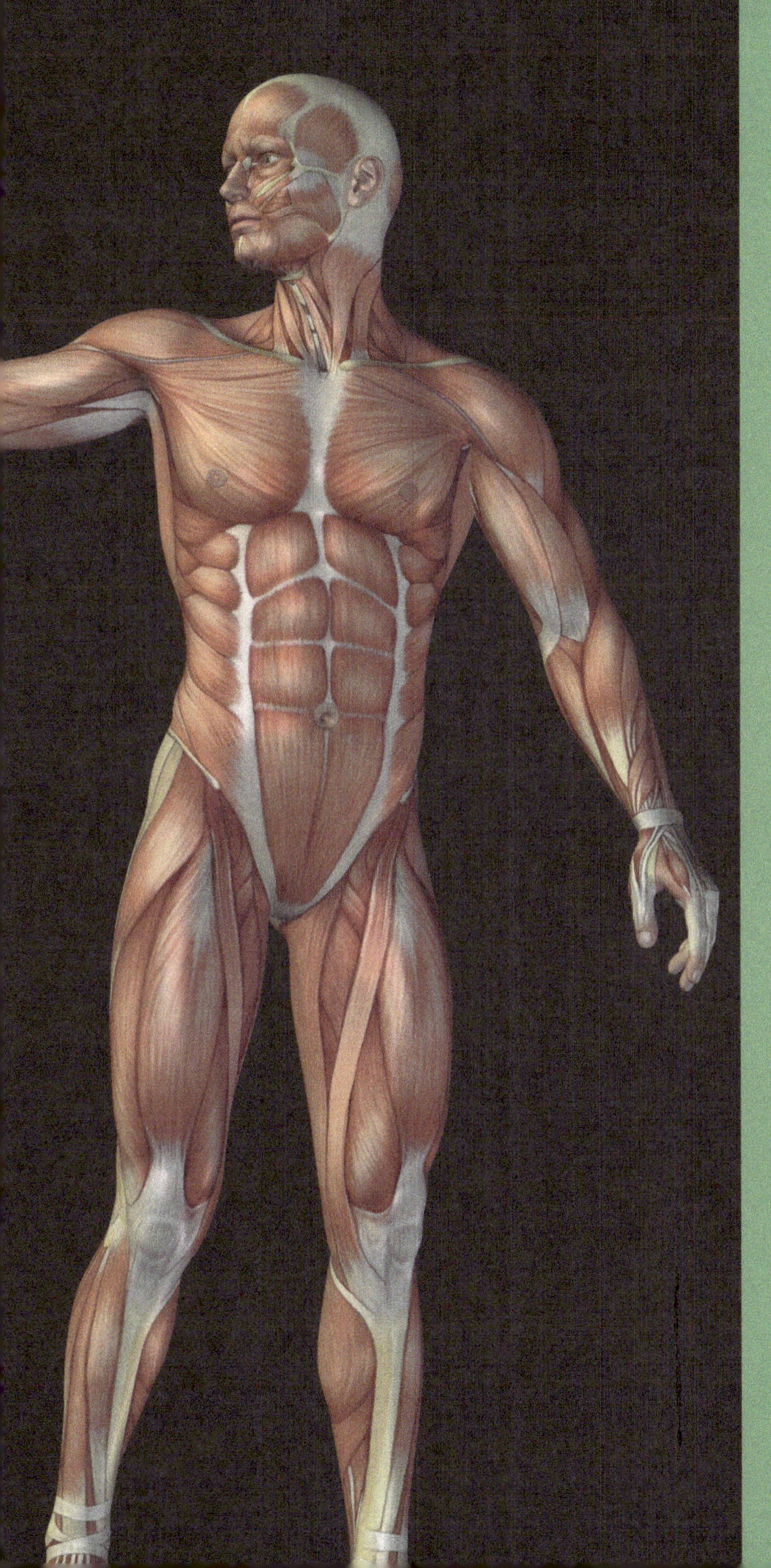

The human body is mainly composed of the head, neck, torso, arms and legs. No body part works in isolation. They work together as each of them performs its functions with the help of the others.

What is human anatomy?

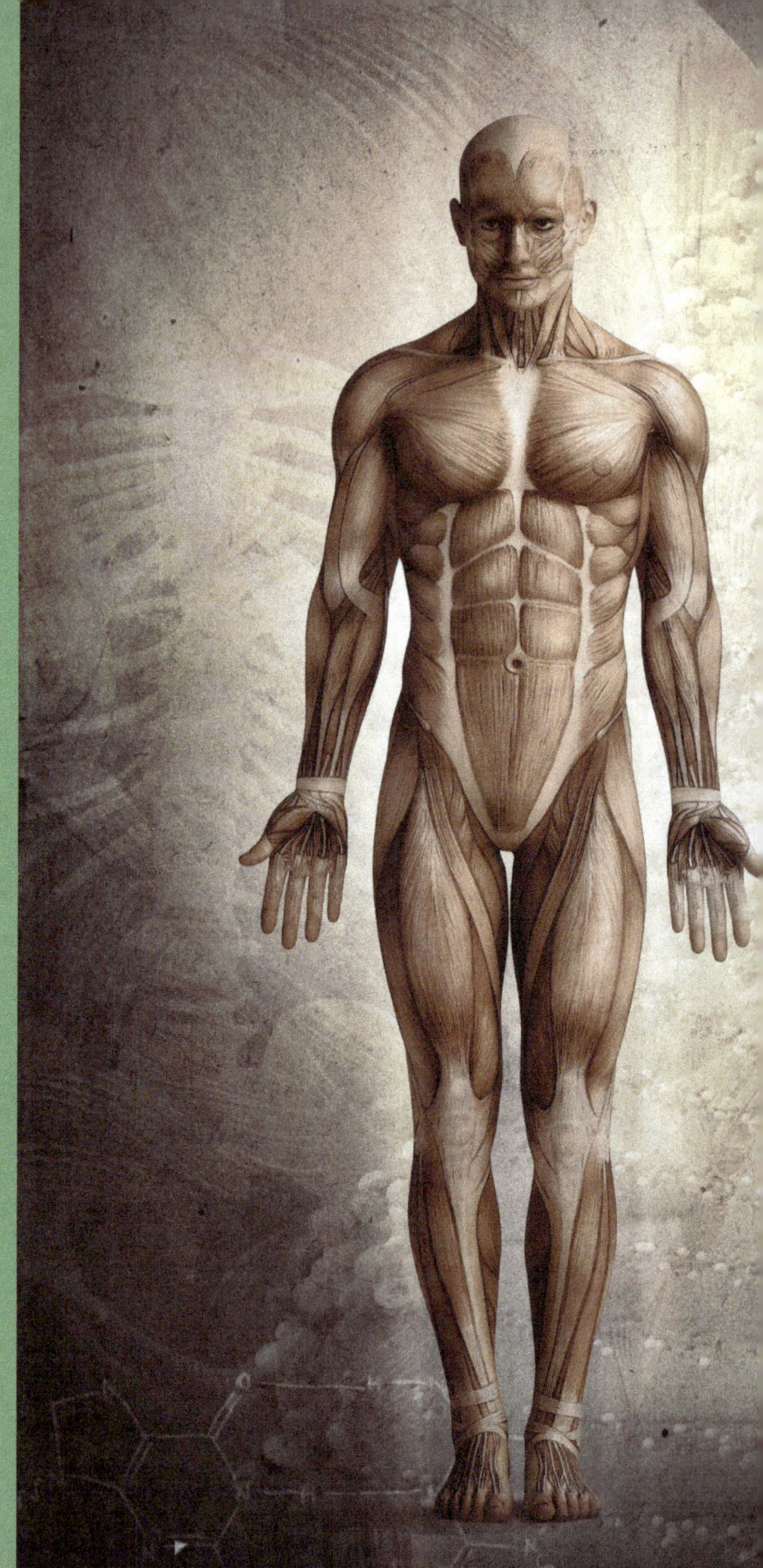

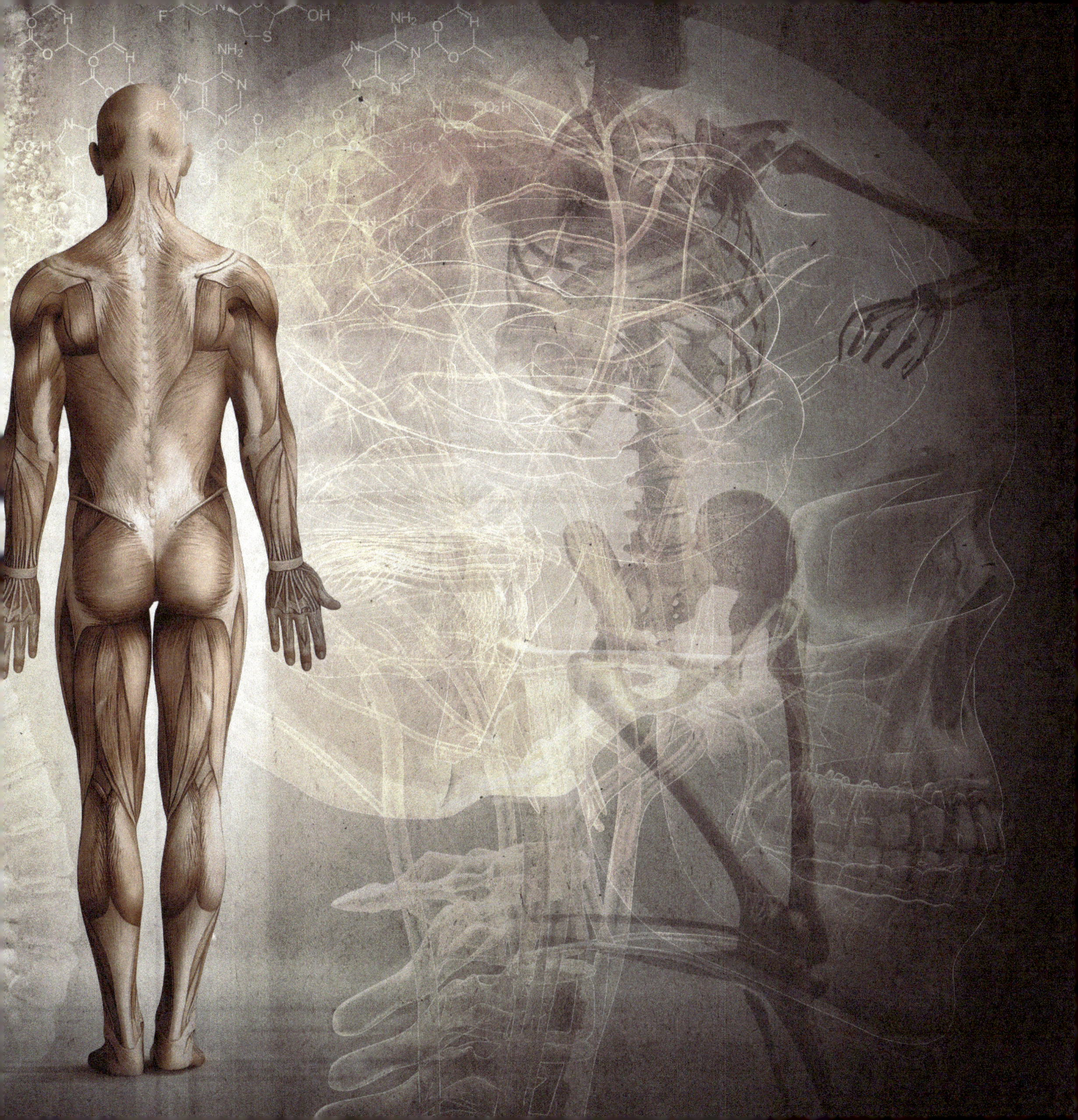

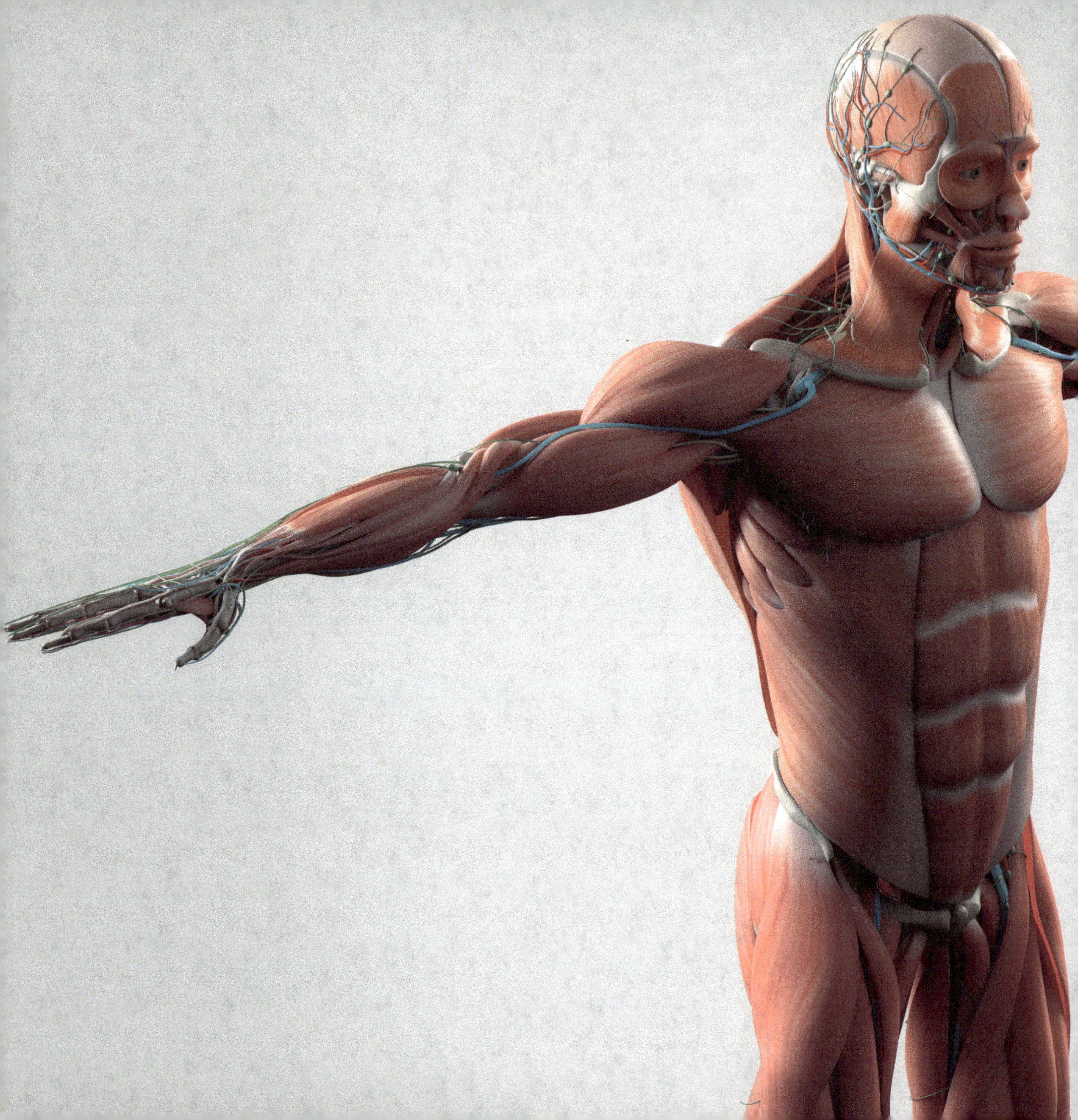

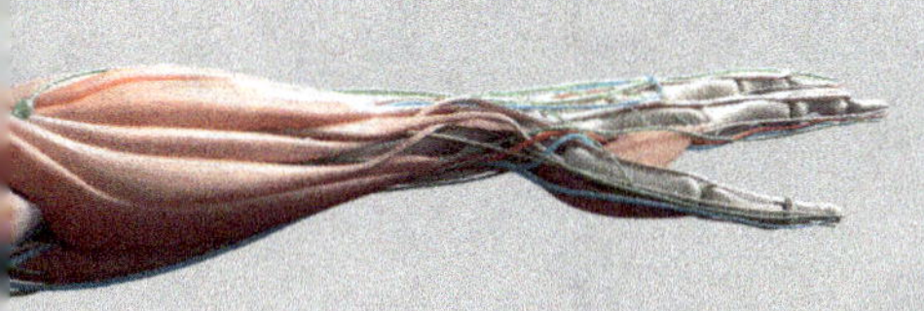

Anatomy is the scientific study of the different systems and organs of the body. Cells are known as the building blocks of human life. The human body is basically composed of cells that form tissues which in turn create organ systems. Each organ of the body performs different functions.

Basic Facts You
Should Know:

- Nearly 100 trillion
cells compose the
human body.

- About 100 billion
nerve cells are in
the human brain.

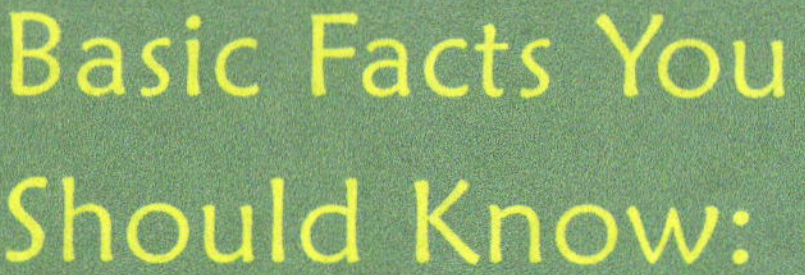

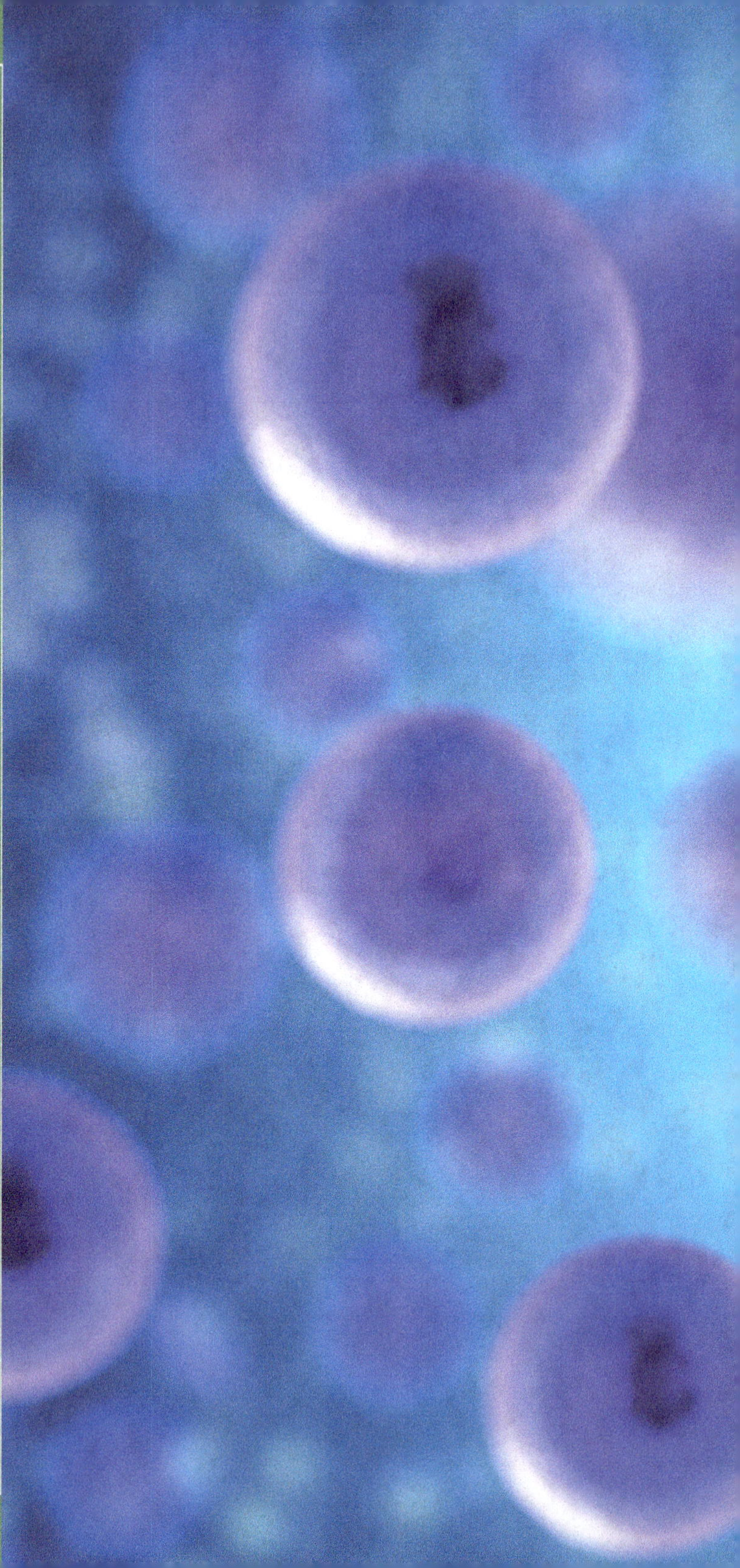

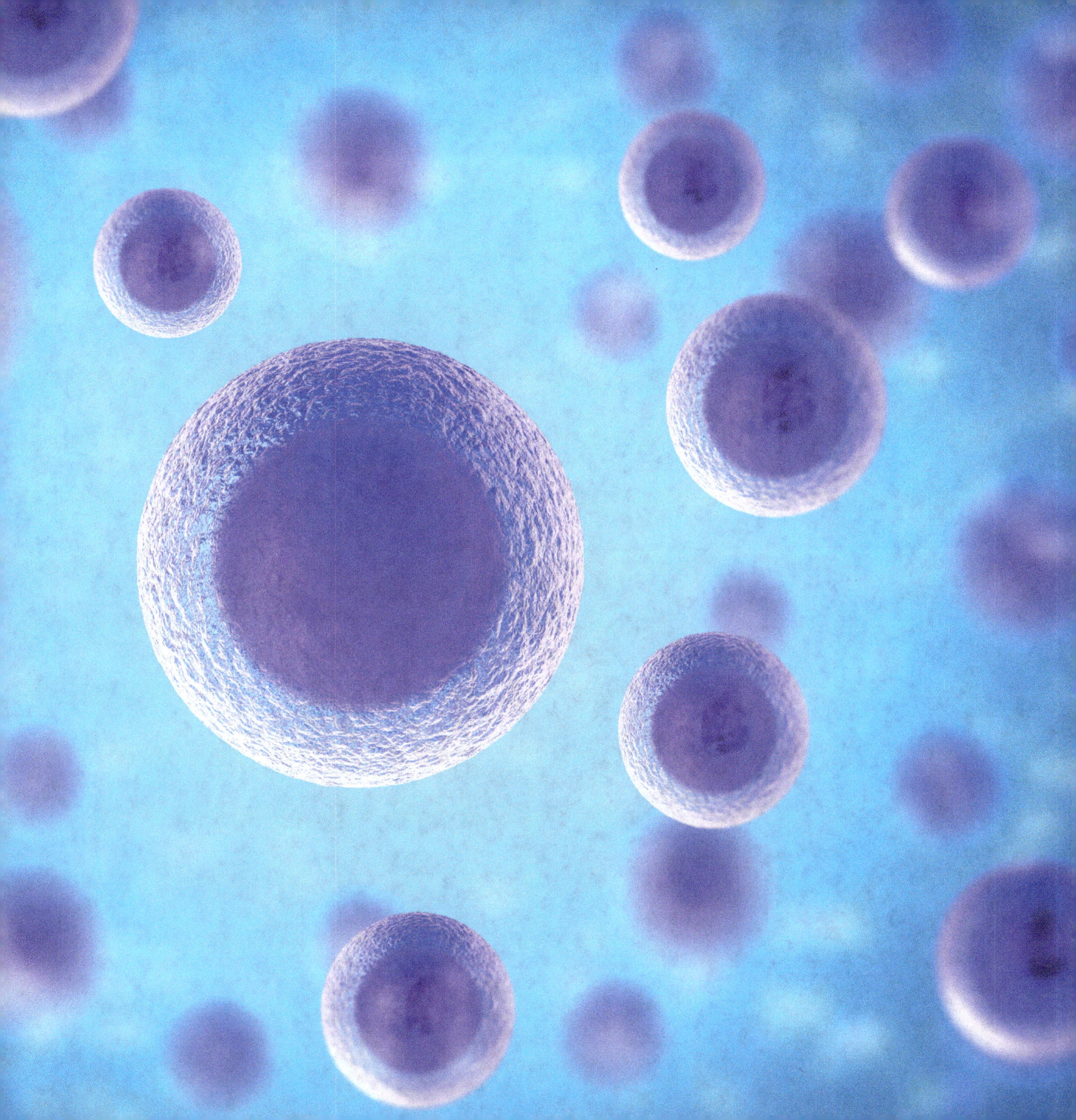

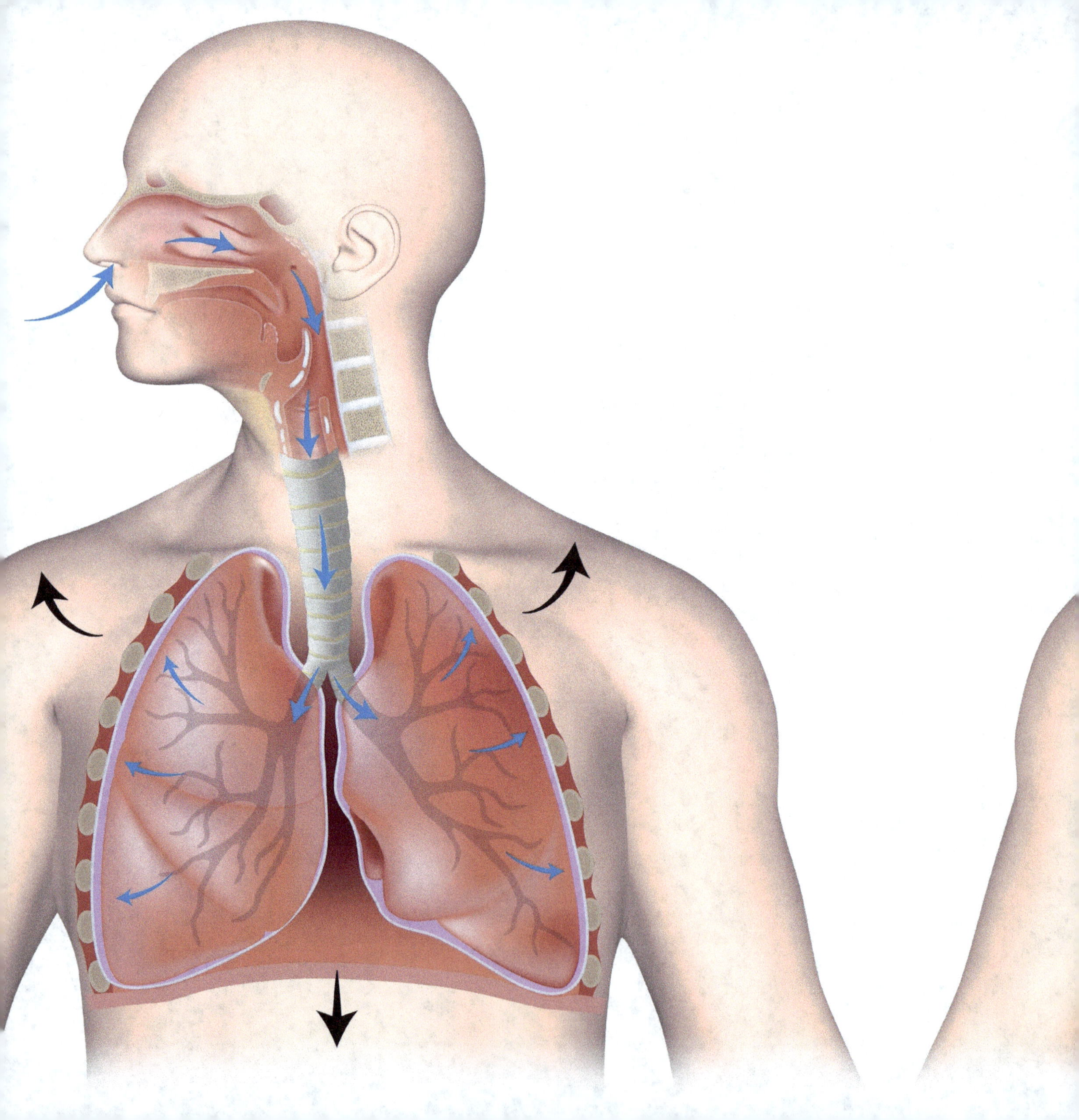

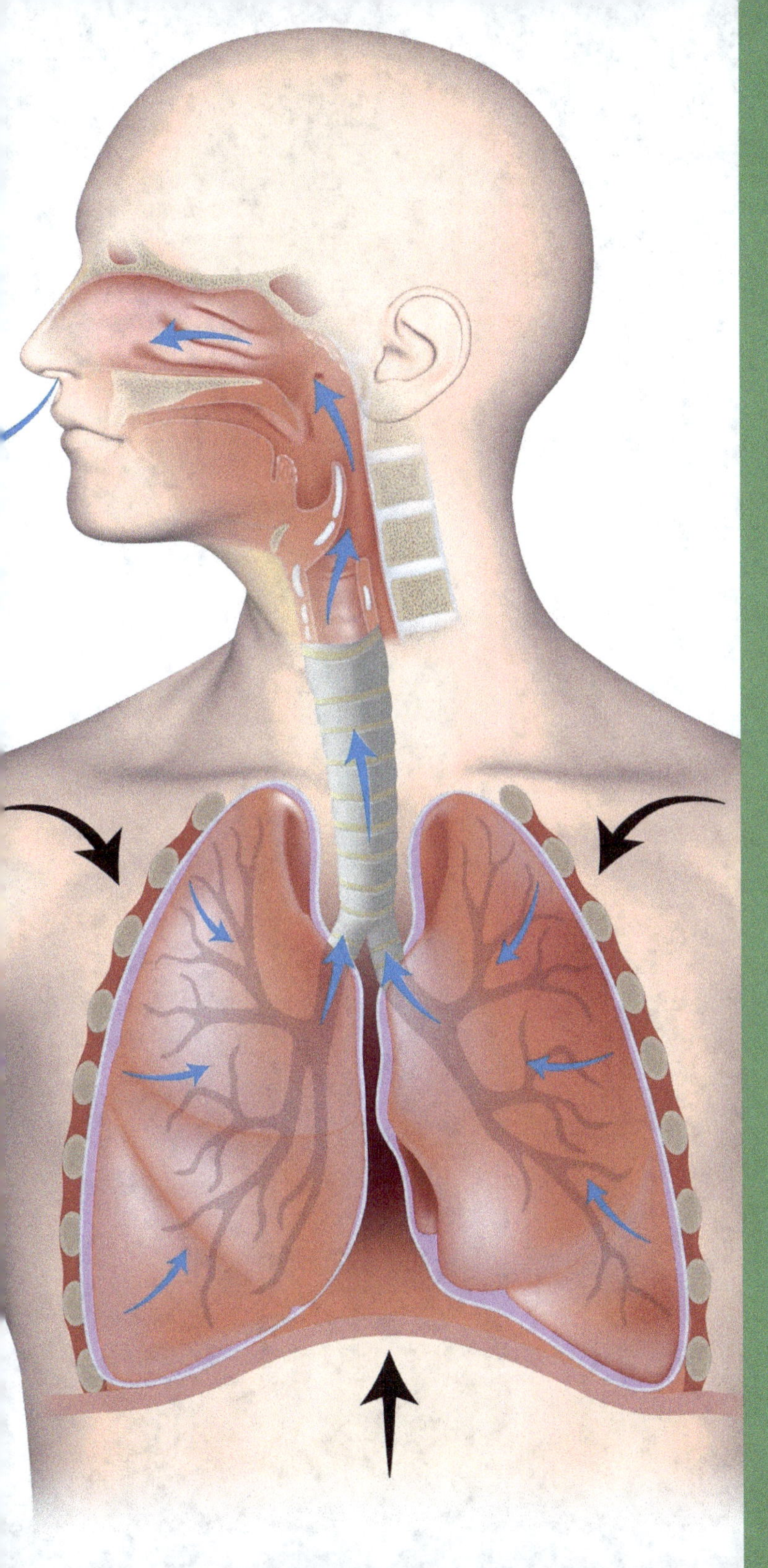

- More than 50% of the average adult's body weight is water.

- An average adult breathes more than 20,000 times a day.

Our body is composed of different organs and systems. They work together so that the human body will function well. Each system works day and night to serve the needs of the human body. These systems support each other, and work together.

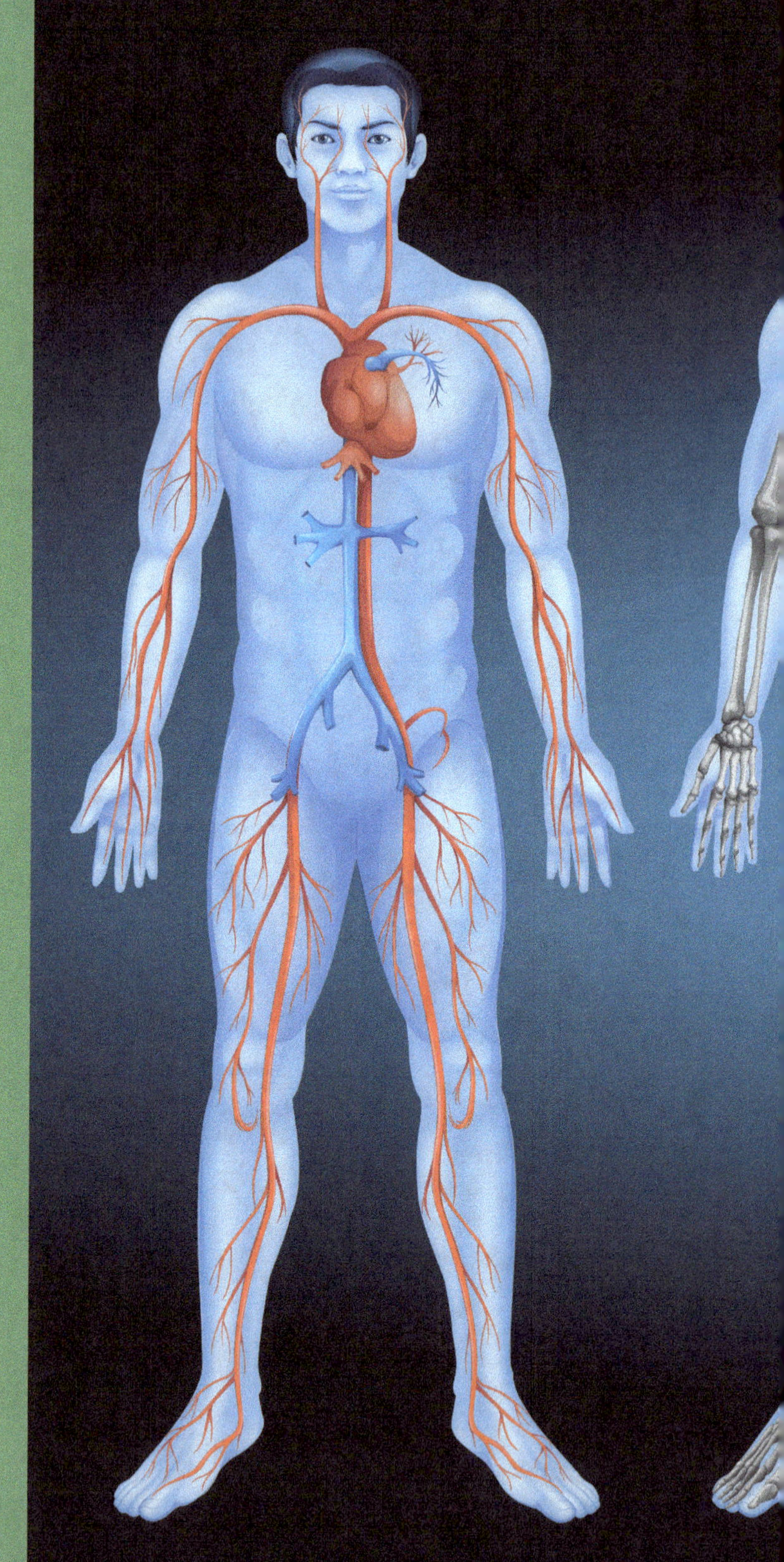

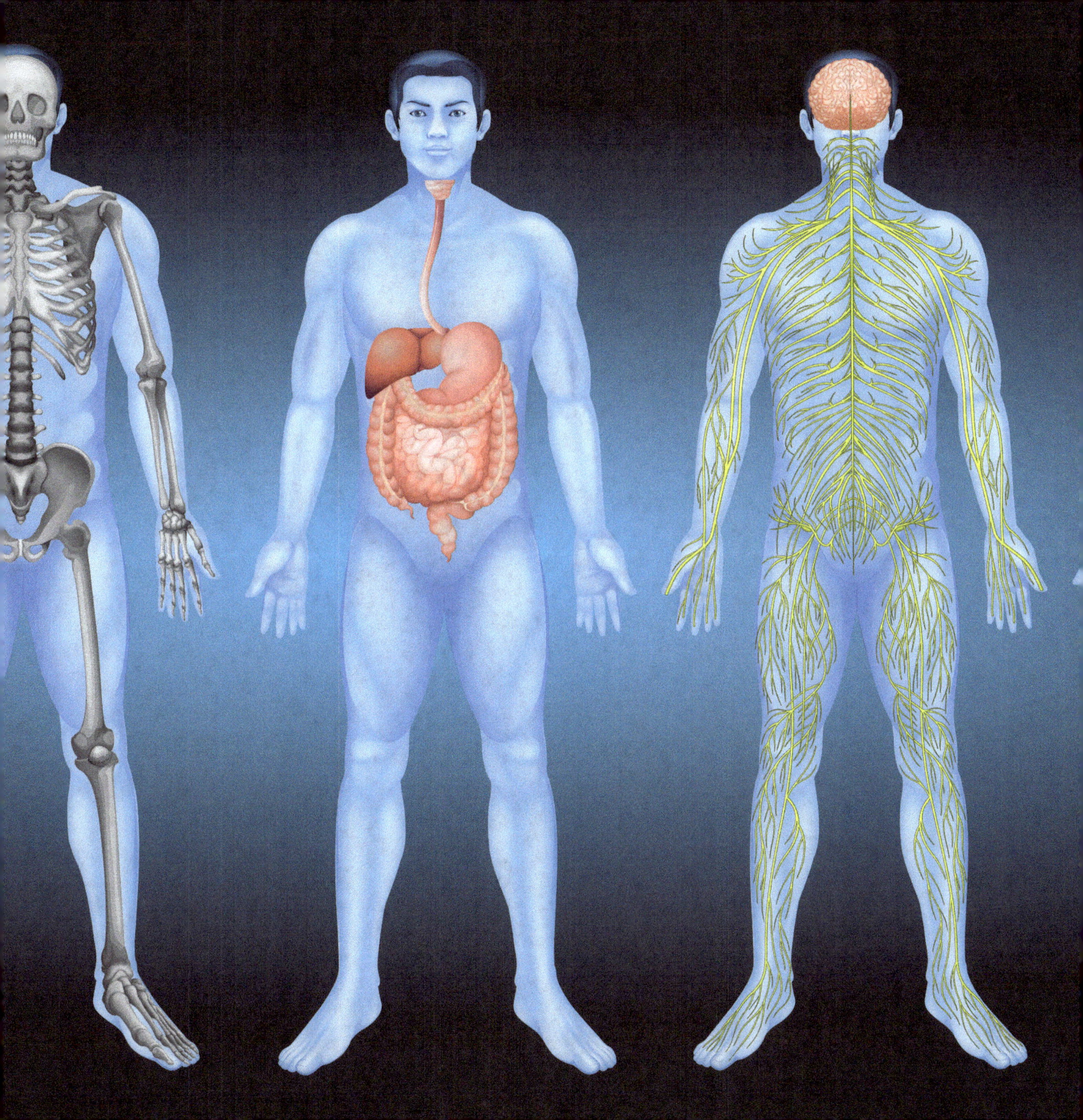

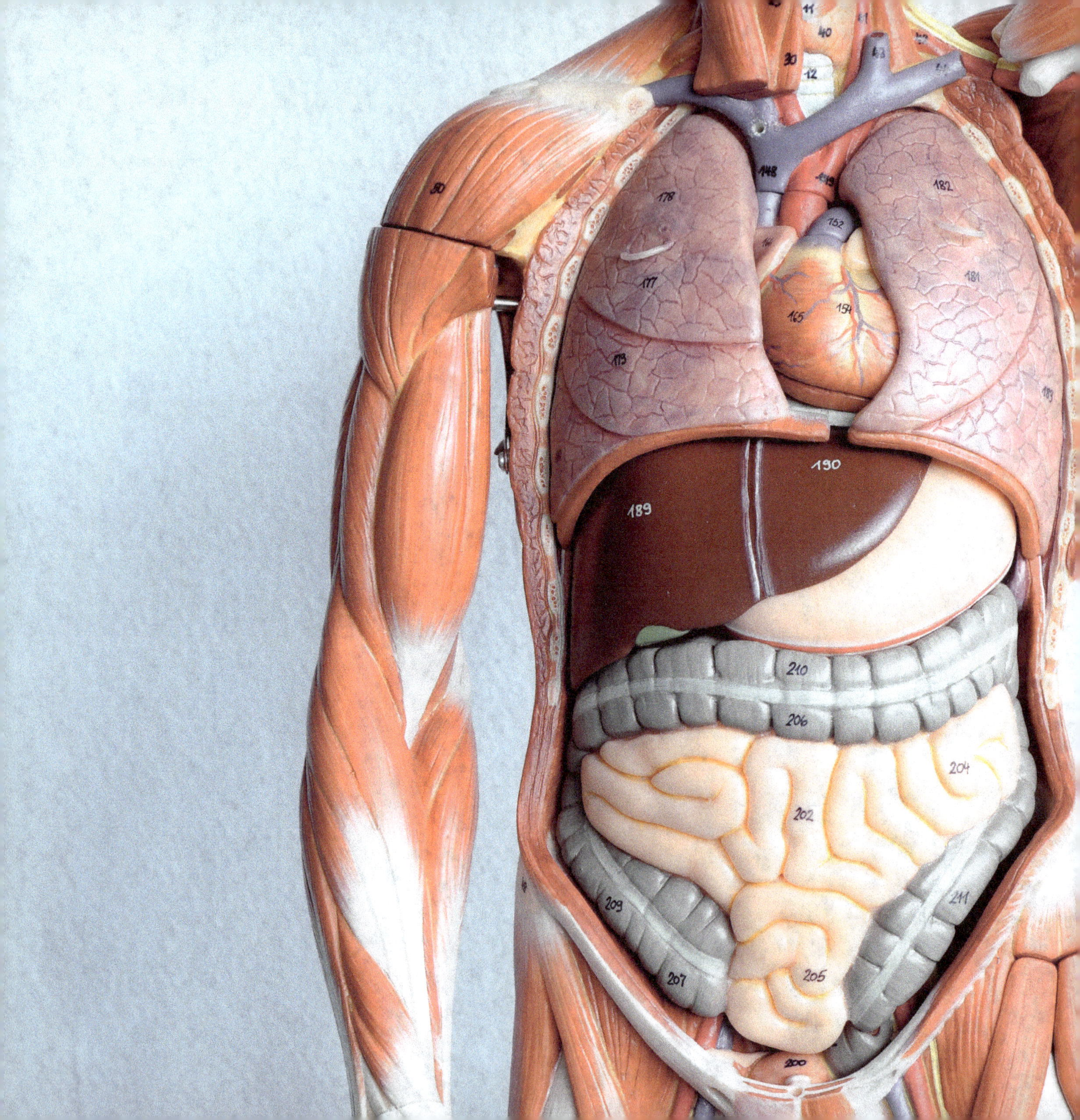

50
178
177
179
148
146
152
181
182
155
154
183
190
189
210
206
204
202
209
211
207
205
200
41
40
30
12
43
44

Let's explore the
vital organs of
the human body
and find out how
they work for
our survival.

The heart pumps
five quarts of blood
through our system.
The size of the
heart depends on
the persons size
and condition.

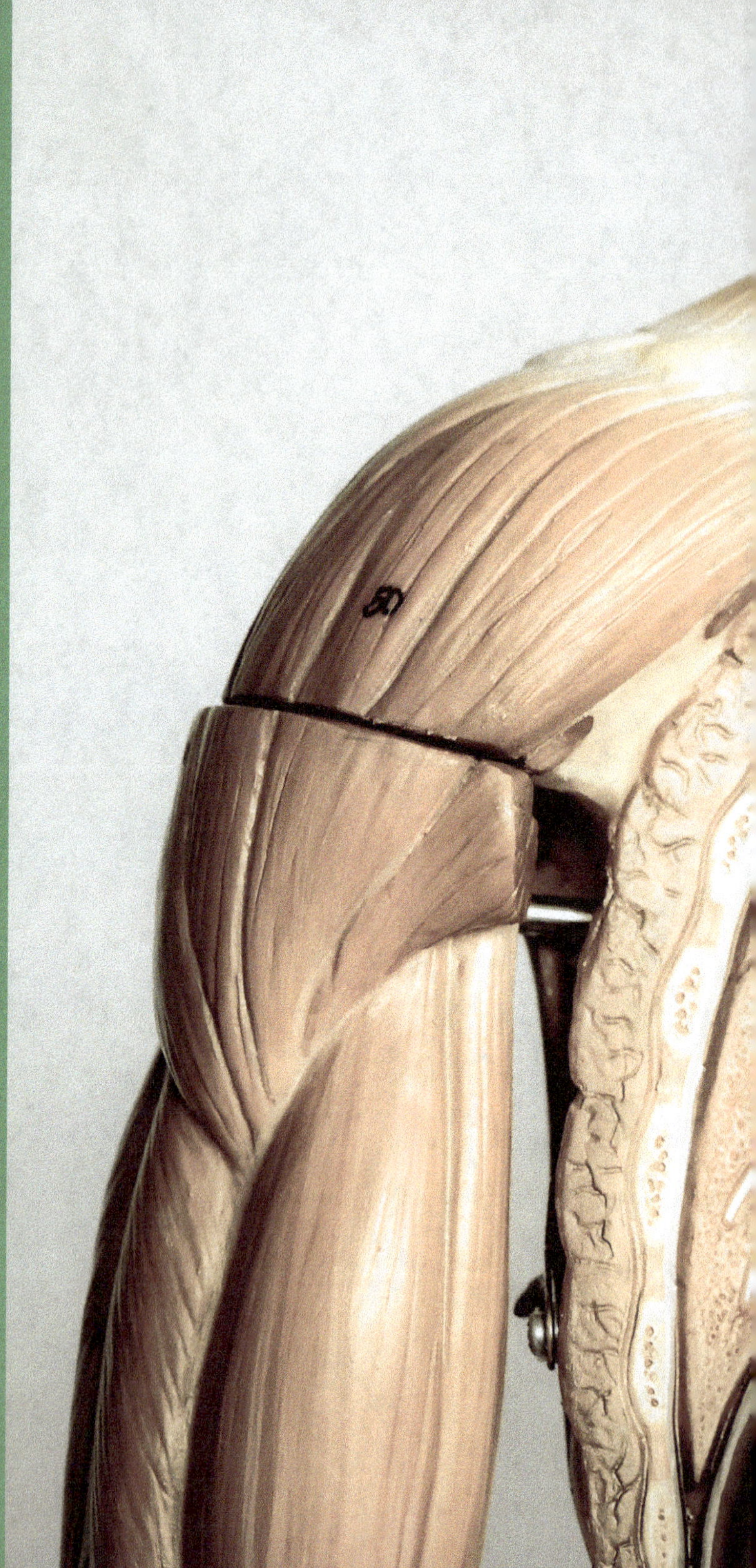

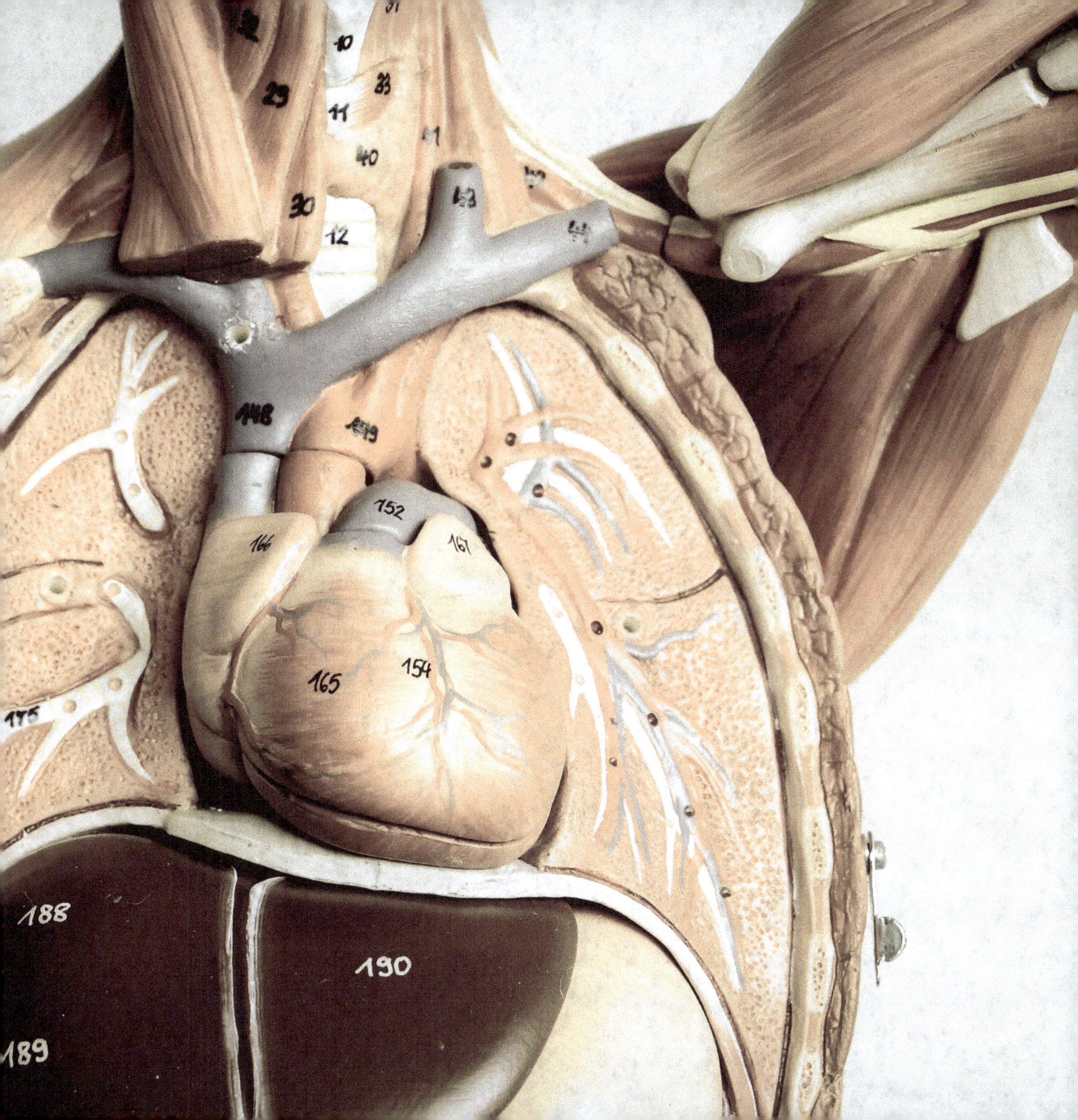
12
10
31
23
33
11
41
40
30
12
53
51
55
54
148
149
152
166
167
165
154
175
188
189
190

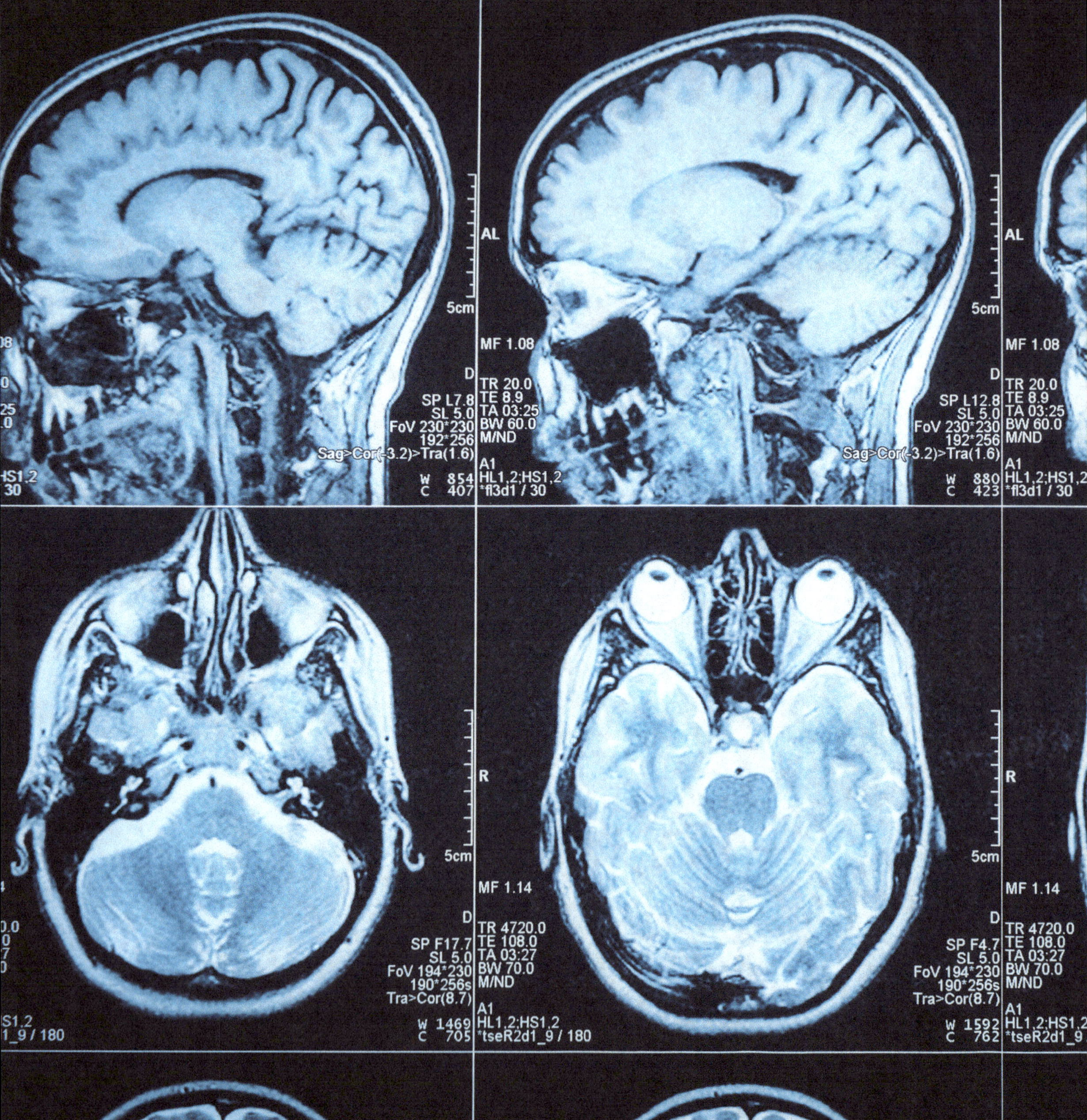
AL
5cm
MF 1.08
D
TR 20.0
TE 8.9
SP L7.8
SL 5.0
TA 03:25
FoV 230*230
BW 60.0
M/ND
192*256
Sag>Cor(-3.2)>Tra(1.6)
A1
W 854
HL1,2;HS1,2
C 407
*fl3d1 / 30
AL
5cm
MF 1.08
D
TR 20.0
TE 8.9
SP L12.8
SL 5.0
TA 03:25
FoV 230*230
BW 60.0
M/ND
192*256
Sag>Cor(-3.2)>Tra(1.6)
A1
W 880
HL1,2;HS1,2
C 423
*fl3d1 / 30
R
5cm
MF 1.14
D
TR 4720.0
TE 108.0
SP F17.7
SL 5.0
TA 03:27
FoV 194*230
BW 70.0
M/ND
190*256s
Tra>Cor(8.7)
A1
W 1469
HL1,2;HS1,2
C 705
*tseR2d1_9 / 180
R
5cm
MF 1.14
D
TR 4720.0
TE 108.0
SP F4.7
SL 5.0
TA 03:27
FoV 194*230
BW 70.0
M/ND
190*256s
Tra>Cor(8.7)
A1
W 1592
HL1,2;HS1,2
C 762
*tseR2d1_9 /

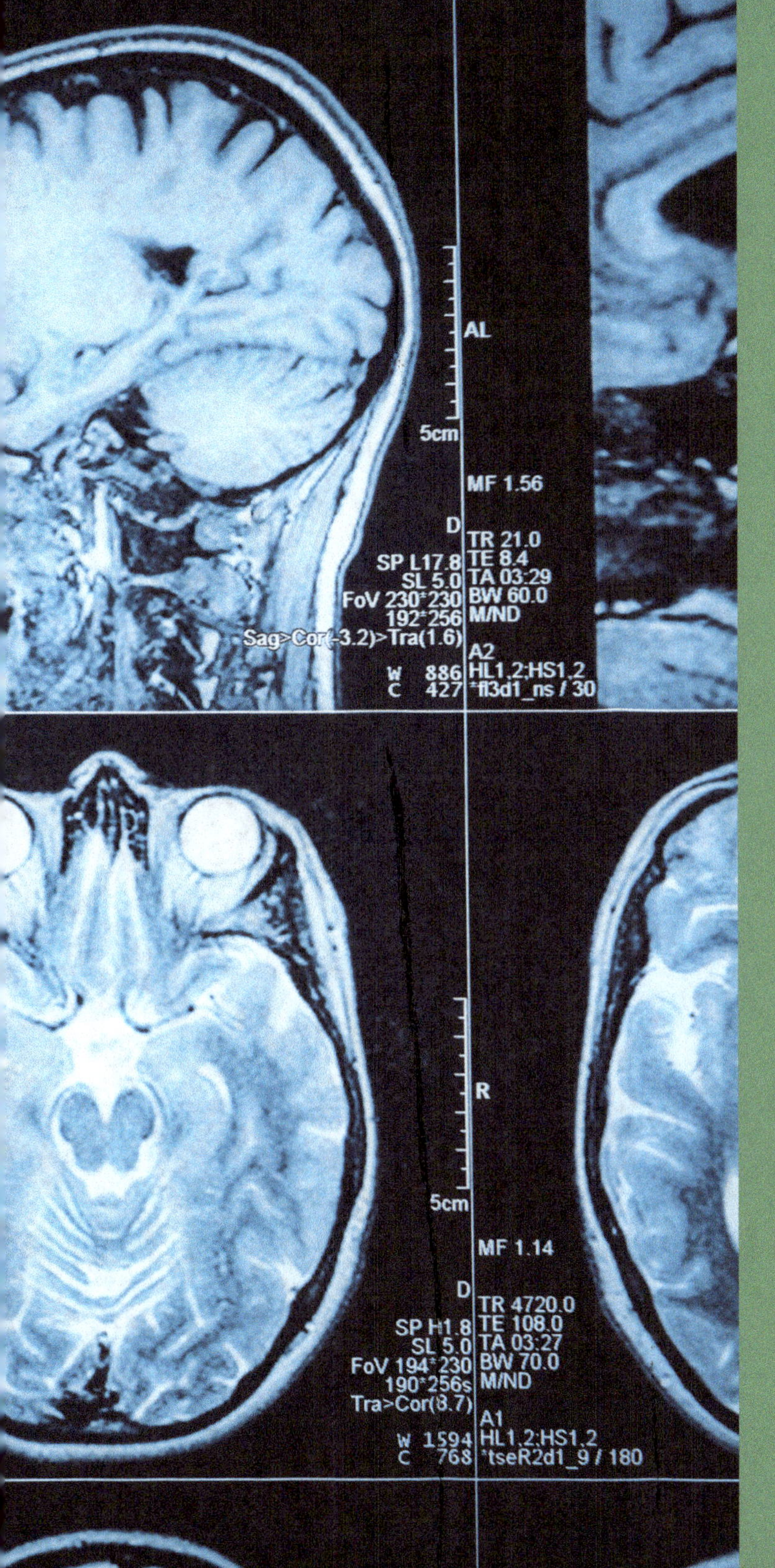

The brain is responsible for all the actions of the systems and the organs of the body. It is composed of billions of cells known as neurons.

The heart is another important organ in your body. It pumps blood so it can circulate in the body. The blood containing carbon dioxide goes to the lungs to exchange that gas for oxygen that it then takes to all the cells.

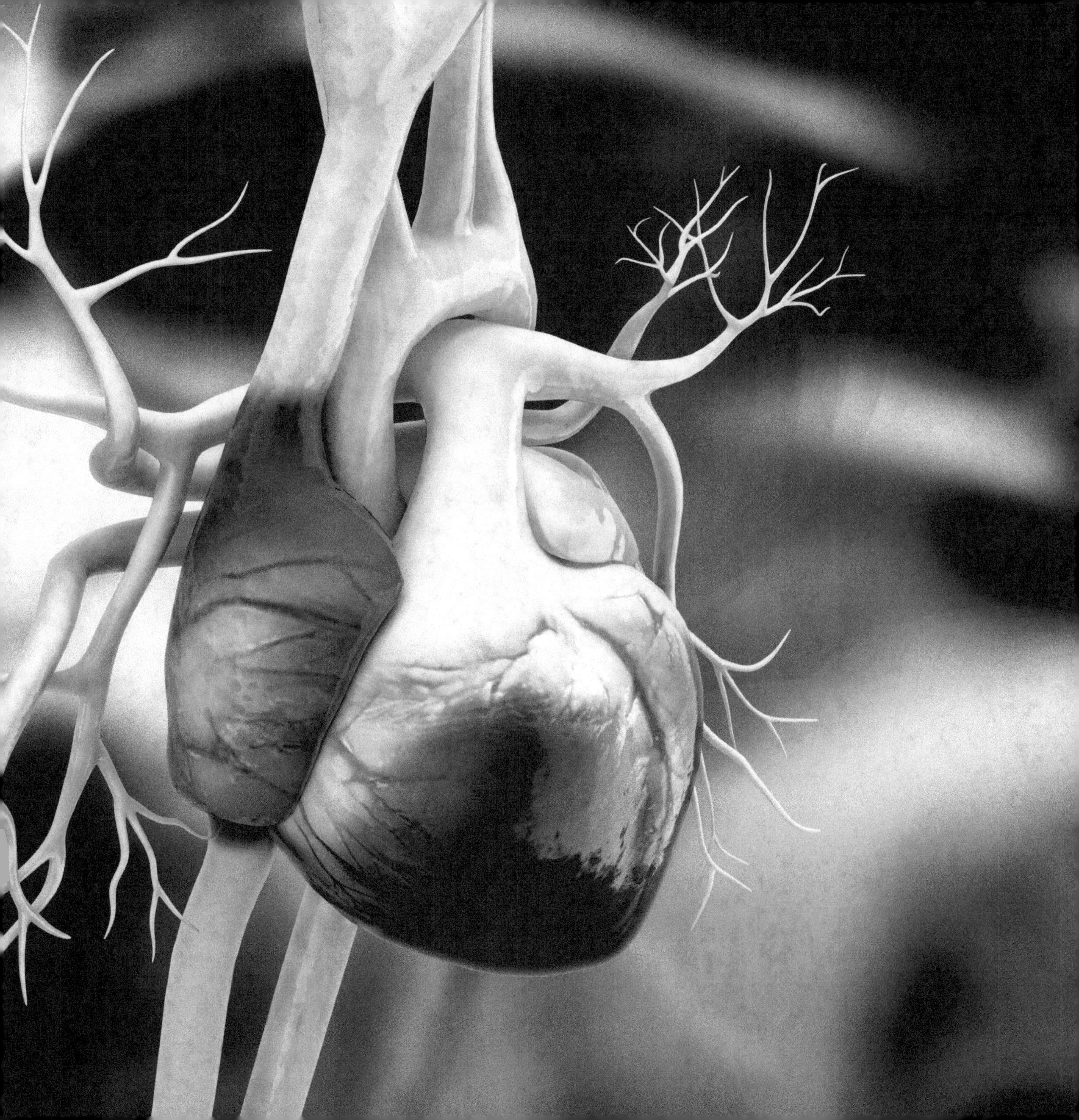

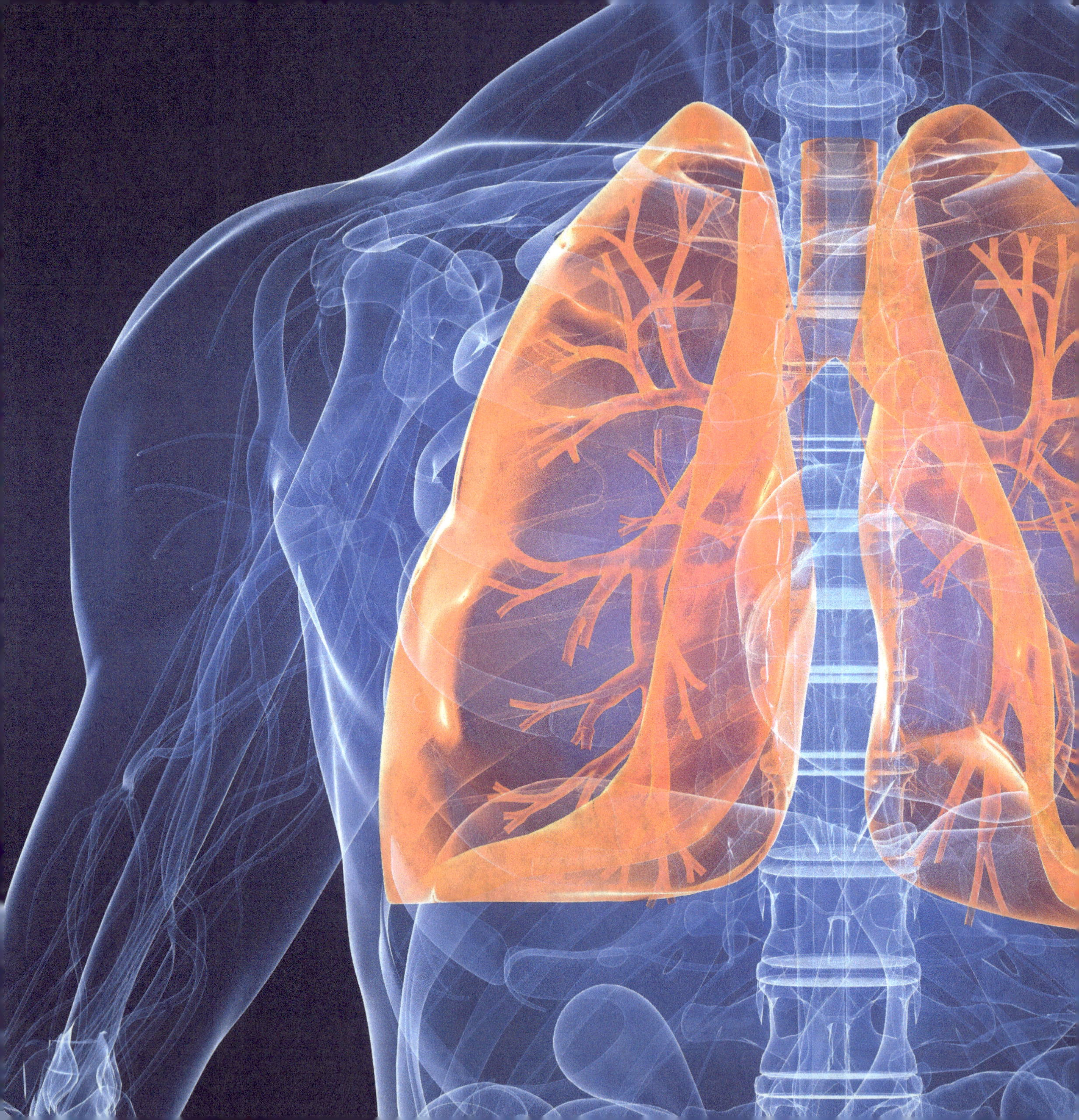

The lungs are the key organs in the respiratory system. They are found on either side of the heart. We inhale to bring oxygen into our lungs, which pass it to our blood system. We breathe out to get rid of the carbon dioxide the blood has delivered.

The liver performs different vital functions.
These include detoxification of food, hormone production, protein synthesis and decomposition of red blood cells.

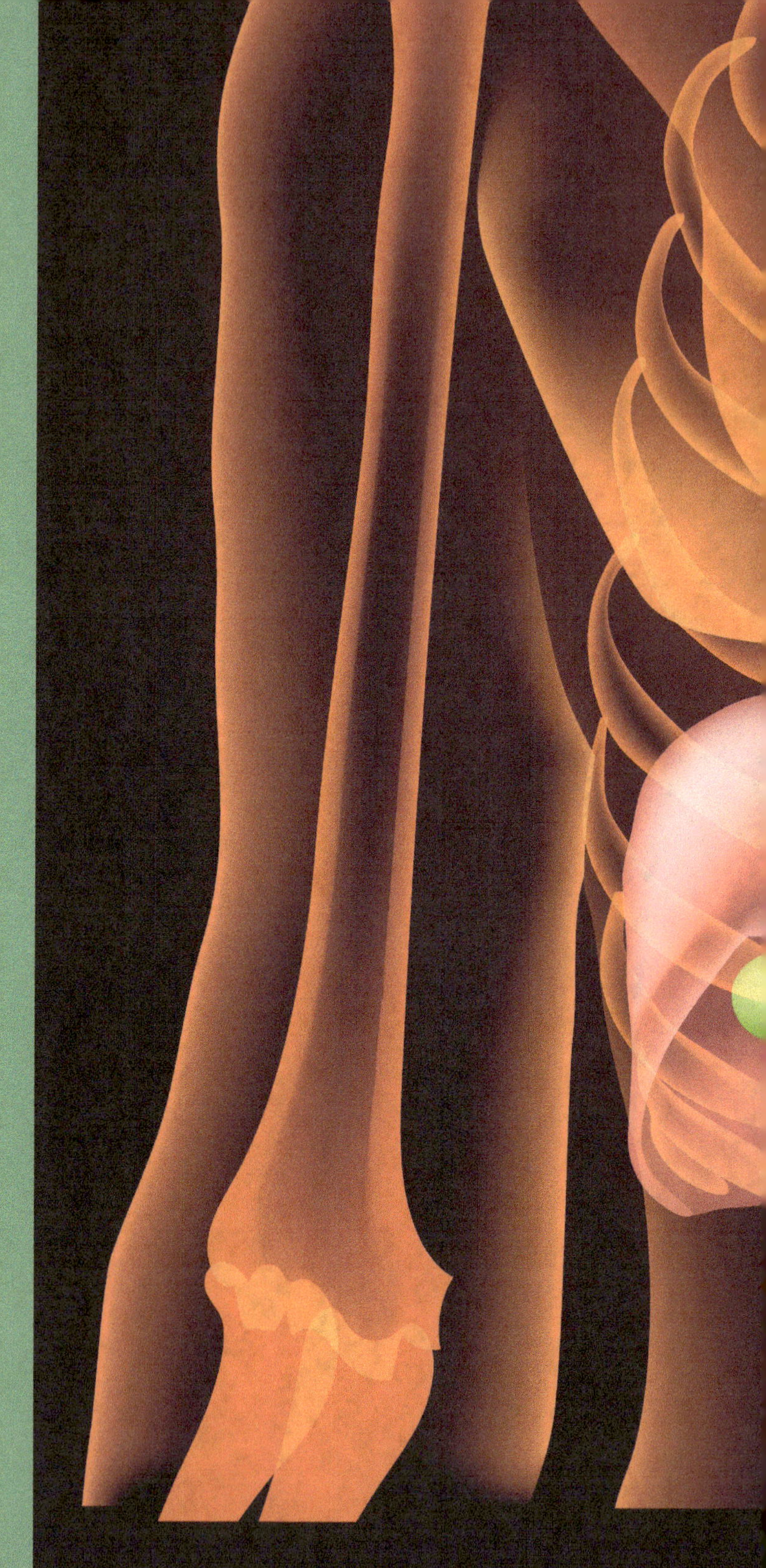

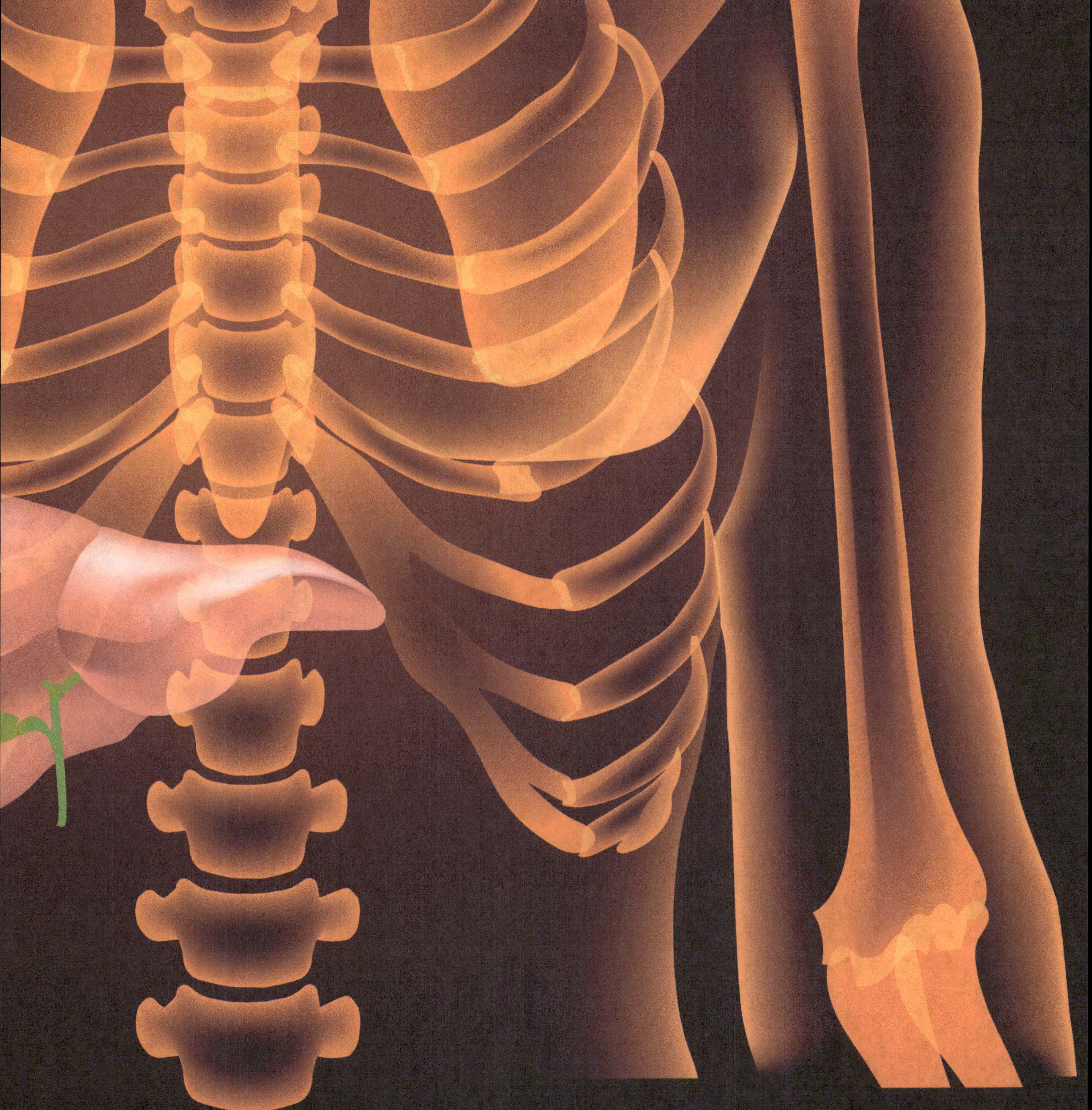

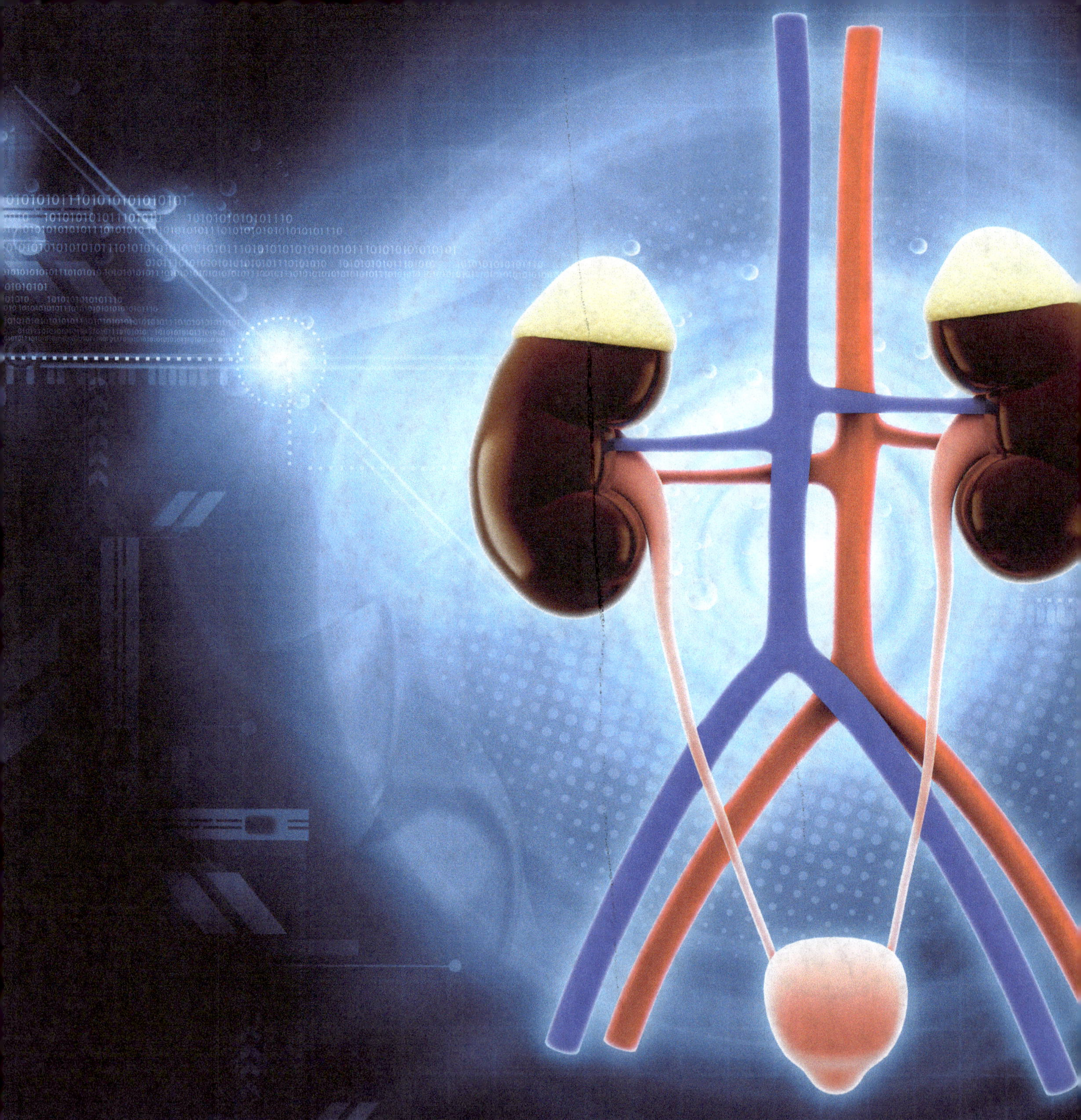

Kidneys. These organs remove waste and extra fluids from the blood. They are the body's cleaners. As the kidneys function, urea is taken out of the blood and combined with water and other substances to form urine.

Stomach. This is an important organ in the digestive system. It is located between the esophagus (the food pipe) and the small intestine. Enzymes, acids and gastric juices are released by the stomach to aid in digestion.

Did you enjoy reading? Share this to your friends.

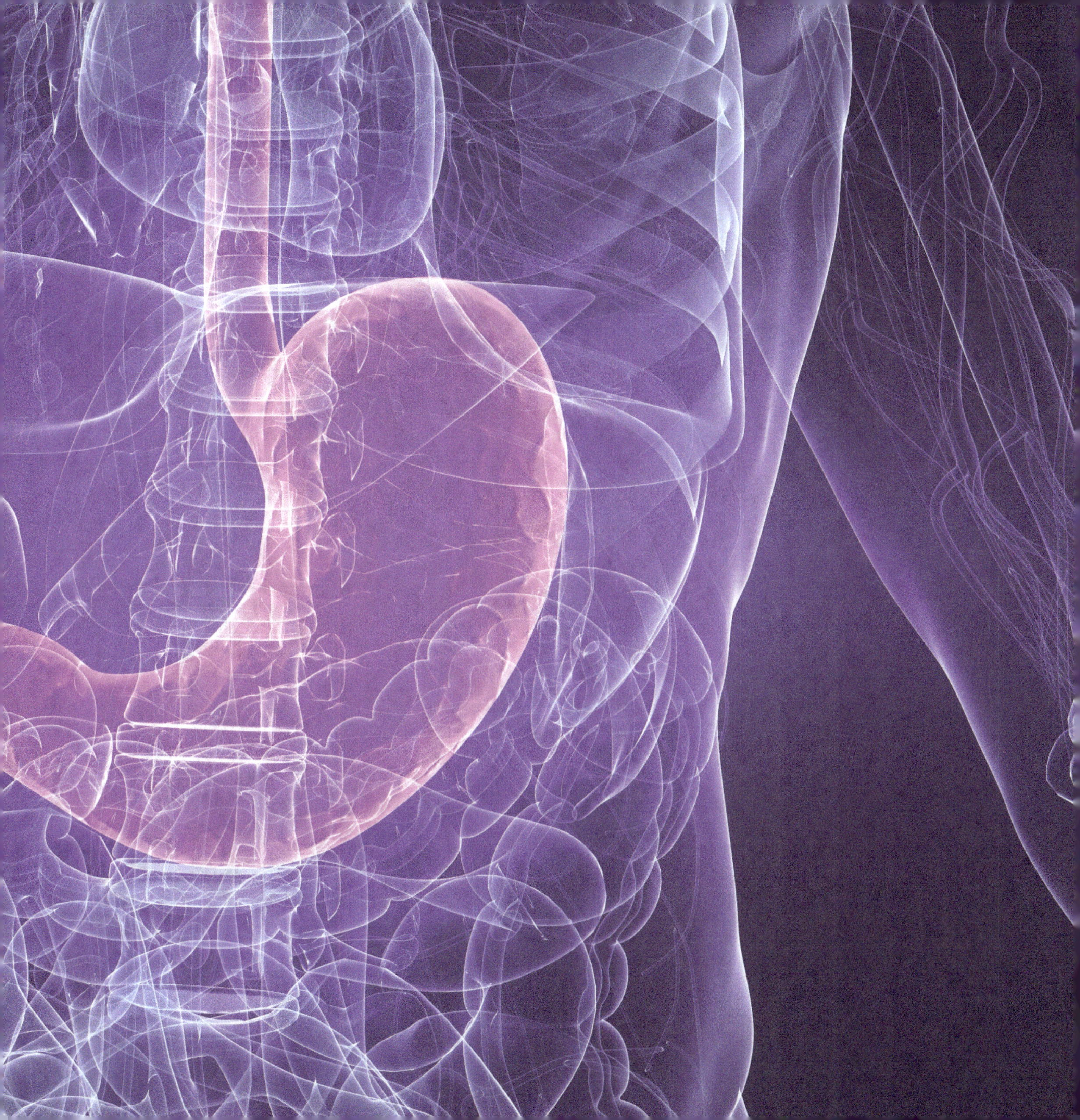

Visit
BABY PROFESSOR
EDUCATION KIDS
www.BabyProfessorBooks.com
to download Free Baby Professor eBooks
and view our catalog of new and exciting
Children's Books